TOP-RATED SHADE GARDENING

This book was produced for Western Publishing Company, Inc., by the staff of Horticultural Associates, Inc.

Executive Producer: Richard M. Ray
Contributing Authors: Alvin Horton, Randy Peterson
Photography: Michael Landis
Art Director: Richard Baker
Book Design and Production: Lingke Moeis
Coordinating Editor: Lance Walheim
Research Editor: Randy Peterson
Copy Editor: Miriam Boucher
Production Editor: Kathleen Parker
Illustrations: Charles Hoeppner
Typography: Linda Encinas
Additional Photography: William Aplin, Susan A. Roth
Cover Photo: Michael Landis
Acknowledgements: Buchart Gardens, Victoria, B.C., CAN; Tom Courtright, Orchard Nursery, Lafayette, CA; Jimmy Grimes, Smyrna, GA; Jim Gibbs, Smyrna, GA; Dana Jones, Atlanta, GA; Japanese Garden Society of Oregon, Portland, OR; Robert Rodler, Huntington, NY.

For Golden Press:
Publisher: Jonathan P. Latimer
Senior Editor: Susan A. Roth
Associate Editor: Karen Stray Nolting

3 Shade Gardening
- 4 What Kind of Shade Do You Have?
- 6 Shade-Loving Plants
- 11 Trees for Casting Shade

13 Designing Shade Gardens
- 13 Texture
- 14 Color
- 15 Focal Points
- 17 Plant Combinations

19 Caring for Shade Gardens
- 20 Climates
- 24 Soil, Water, Fertilizer, and Mulch
- 25 Air and Light

29 Top-Rated Plants for Shady Gardens
- 30 Annuals, Perennials, and Bulbs
- 40 Wildflowers and Ferns
- 44 Shrubs, Vines, and Ground Covers
- 58 Lawn Grasses
- 59 Understory Trees
- 63 Index

 Golden Press • New York
Western Publishing Company, Inc.
Racine, Wisconsin

Copyright © 1984 by Horticultural Associates, Inc.
All rights reserved. Produced in the U.S.A.
Library of Congress Catalog Card Number 82-83055
Golden® and Golden Press® are trademarks of Western Publishing Company, Inc.
ISBN 0-307-46628-0

At left: A meandering path leads to a cool, rustic retreat created by a vine-covered arbor.

Shade Gardening

On a sweltering summer day when even the roses are drooping, a shady garden spot can offer a delightfully cool retreat. It may be 90°F on the lawn, but beneath the spreading branches of an oak tree, the temperature is likely to be a welcome 75°F. That same oak, casting its cooling shade on the house, will keep the indoor temperatures down also.

Shade means comfort—comfort to people and comfort to plants. Though shady spots in many a yard are unsightly barren patches of ground, it doesn't have to be so. The comfort you find in the shade is an equal comfort to countless beautiful garden plants. If you have considered the shady areas of your yard impossible to garden in, it's time to explore some possibilities. Shade offers special gardening opportunities that are diverse and exciting. This book is designed to help you discover and make the most of them.

Masses of sherbet-colored tuberous begonias (*Begonia x tuberhybrida*) or white impatiens (*Impatiens wallerana*) could brighten beds beneath trees or around a shaded patio. You can decorate a dimly lit wall with the heavy flower clusters of Chinese jasmine (*Jasminum polyanthum*) and enjoy their spicy fragrance on a sultry summer evening. Under a grove of trees, instead of an expanse of fallen leaves, you can plant groups of azaleas (*Rhododendron* species), daffodils (*Narcissus* species), and crocus (*Crocus* species) to put on an unmatched display in spring.

Gardening in the shade does require some know-how. Knowing

Periwinkle (*Vinca minor*)

Clematis (*Clematis* sp.)

Viburnum (*Viburnum* sp.)

Kurume azalea (*Rhododendron* hybrid)

Many choices are open to the gardener when grouping plants in dappled shade.

Small spaces can achieve grand effects when plants are grown under the light shade cast by an overhead lath screen.

Cool beds of maidenhair fern (*Adiantum pedatum*) add greenery along a brick walkway in the bright open shade on the north side of a house.

what kind of shade you are dealing with—not all shade is the same— knowing which plants will do well there, and knowing how to plant and care for them properly are the only secrets. This book will give you all that know-how. And it presents more than 300 kinds of shade-loving plants for you to choose among.

WHAT KIND OF SHADE DO YOU HAVE?

Not all shade is alike. Shade may be cast by the branches of a tall tree or be caused by the shadow of a building. Some shady spots change dramatically with the seasons and others do not. The plants you choose and the gardening techniques that make gardening in the shade a success depend upon understanding the kind of shade you have.

The sources and qualities of shade are many, but it's possible to describe shade as four general types: light shade, open shade, half-shade, and deep shade. Each type represents, of course, a range rather than a single degree of shade. These key terms are used throughout this book to guide you in evaluating the quality of shade in your garden and in selecting suitable shade-loving plants.

Light shade: Frequently described as dappled shade, light shade is encountered beneath the branches of high-branched, open trees. Trees with finely divided foliage, such as thornless honey locust (*Gleditsia triacanthos inermis*) or silk tree (*Albizia julibrissin*), cast dappled shade. Other trees can be pruned and the branches thinned so they cast light shade. Weak direct sunlight may shine fully on this area early in the morning and late in the afternoon, but during the rest of the day the ground is dappled with the constantly changing pattern of shadow and light that filters through the gaps in the foliage overhead.

Lightly shaded areas are usually cool and they are often moister than deeply shaded areas because rainfall can reach the ground. If tree roots are surface ones, then soil improvement, watering, and fertilizing will increase the vigor of any plants you grow there.

A wide range of both green and flowering plants can be grown in dappled shade. Enchanting woodland gardens with paths and perhaps even a babbling brook are naturals in large areas of dappled shade. On the more formal side, you can choose an Oriental style setting or a traditional one with beds of flowering plants.

Open shade: North sides of houses, tall evergreen windbreaks, or walls and narrow side yards are usually in shadow year round, however they may receive considerable reflected light because the area is open to the sky. The area beneath a roof overhang may also be similarly shaded. This kind of bright shade is called open shade since the area is open to the sky. If nearby walls or pavement are light colored, considerable additional brightness is caught by these areas.

Air circulation and rainfall are often excellent in these areas, offering wonderful possibilities for successful gardening. Almost all shade plants thrive in bright open shade, except those that require some direct sun for a few hours of the day.

Deep shade: This is the darkest shade for gardening. No direct sunlight falls on the ground, except perhaps briefly very early or late in the day. Indirect or reflected light is also limited. Deep shade is found year round beneath dense evergreen trees such as Southern magnolias (*Magnolia grandiflora*), hemlocks (*Tsuga* species), and some pines (*Pinus* species). The thickly foliaged and low branching trees such as beech (*Fagus* species) and Norway maple (*Acer platanoides*) cast deep shade, but only in summer. Because they drop their leaves for the winter, full sun shines in these areas part of the year.

atrium

Though shady spots are often thought of as cool, moist spots, deeply shaded areas beneath trees are often dry because the dense canopy of foliage acts as an umbrella, preventing rain from reaching the ground. The greedy surface roots of many kinds of trees also rob the topsoil of moisture and nutrients.

Deeply shaded areas are most frequently areas that are bare of ground-covering plants. Though there isn't enough light to grow flowering plants in deep shade, many ferns and ground covers will flourish there, if the ground is kept watered and fertilized. It also helps if the soil is improved. The plants that do best in deep shade are often shallowed-rooted creeping kinds that are native woodland plants—these are naturals for competing successfully with tree roots.

Early-spring-flowering bulbs can be a beautiful addition to areas beneath deciduous trees, which are deeply shaded only in summer. Bulbs will do well there especially if the trees are late-leafing kinds. The bulbs bloom and their foliage has time to bask in full sunlight before the trees' leaves emerge to shade the already withering foliage.

Half-shade: This is a combination of full sun for part of the day and open or deep shade during the rest of the day. Half-shade is often found on the east or west sides of a house that are fairly open to the sky. Full morning sun may fall on the east side of the house, however, as the sun moves across the sky, the house's shadow will transform the sunny spot into a shaded spot. And on the west side of a house, just the opposite happens, with the area being in shadow in the morning and brightly lit in the afternoon.

Some people don't even think of these half-shade spots as problem spots, because so many plants do well there. Which plants flourish in half-shade depends upon the degree of direct sun and the deepness of the shade. If the area is brightly lit for at least four hours, even some sun-loving plants will do fairly well there, though they may not flower as much as they would if grown in all-day sun.

In actuality, these simple definitions of shade aren't so clear cut. The amount of light that falls on any part of your garden is modified by your climate. One climate factor is latitude: sun—and shade—is brighter in Atlanta than in Montreal. Another factor is altitude: shade is brighter in mile-high Denver than in Kansas City. Relative humidity even affects the strength of the sunshine: summer shade is brighter in dry El Paso than in muggy, hazy New Orleans.

Still another important factor is the percentage of sunny days during the growing season in your area. Regional variations are dramatic. For example, in June, Seattle has 49 percent sunshine but Fresno has 95 percent. In such places as Seattle, shade is more of a challenge than it is an asset because even open and light-shade areas are gloomy when the sky is cloudy.

Within your garden, mini-variations in the environment can affect the way shade treats your plants. White or light-colored surfaces reflect more light and make the surrounding area brighter. In dry, windy spots a given amount of sunlight may burn shade-loving plants that might benefit from the same amount of sunlight in cooler, more humid spots.

To understand the shade in your garden, observe the different shaded areas carefully through the seasons. The way climate affects shade gardening is discussed in more detail beginning on page 20.

Don't overlook the fact that as a garden grows and young trees mature into stately giants—or even when a fence is put up by the next-door neighbor—shade changes. As it does, you will most likely have to make adjustments—either remove or prune trees or replant with more suitable plant material.

Deciduous trees provide a sheltering canopy of cooling shade in spring and summer, encouraging healthy growth of azaleas and other shade-loving plants.

Different levels of shade intensity are found in every garden, making it possible to create distinctive settings within the landscape.

A shaded path and flowering plants turn this dim spot into a cool retreat.

Flowering dogwood (Cornus sp.) is an effective understory tree, putting on a brilliant floral show in spring.

SHADE-LOVING PLANTS

There are few obvious differences between shade-loving plants and sun-loving plants. Each shade plant has evolved in some degree of shade and is at home there, just as a sun plant is at home in the sun. Some shade plants have broad leaves, to gather as much light as possible. Others simply have leaves that are very light-sensitive—these are usually thin and are susceptible to drying out.

Placed in more shade than it prefers, a flowering plant produces fewer blossoms or fails to bloom at all. At best, it becomes a foliage plant that merely tolerates that degree of shade. Placed in too much shade, any plant—even a shade-loving plant—will weaken as it stretches toward light. Its stems elongate and become spindly. Vigor declines. Eventually the plant dies.

Shade-loving plants prefer coolness. The lower temperature that is part of shade is as important to them as is the lower light intensity. Shade from a tree canopy is particularly cooling—often 15°F or more cooler than nearby sunny spots—because as moisture evaporates from tree leaves it takes heat with it. The air is cool and fresh beneath the canopy of a tree. Shade plants love it. They also love the cooling effect of grass and ground covers growing in the sun surrounding the shaded areas. These may be 10° to 14°F cooler than bare soil would be in the same location, and are even cooler than dark paved surfaces.

Shade-loving plants are quick to suffer from overheating. Good air circulation without dryness helps to counteract the ill effects of high temperatures, but hot, dry air is particularly damaging. Lightly shaded areas in dappled light beneath trees are often more cool and humid than open-shade areas, especially if shade is cast by a building and there is pavement nearby. These differences can mean a different choice of plants for the two areas.

Even if your garden is shady, you don't have to surrender it to solid greenery, unless that is what you really want. Shade gives you the opportunity to enjoy special flowers such as tuberous begonia (*Begonia x tuberhybrida*), monkshood (*Aconitum carmichaelii*), and foxglove (*Digitalis purpurea*), which don't tolerate full sun. There is a wide choice of shade-loving varieties of flowering and evergreen shrubs, small flowering trees, flowering annuals, perennials, bulbs, ferns, and ground covers that flourish in lightly shaded and half-shaded garden sites. Open shade caters to a wide selection of plants too, but those that do well in deep shade are fewer.

ANNUALS

Annuals are plants that grow from seed, produce flowers, set seed and then die in a single growing season. In general, because they require so much energy to complete their life cycle in such a short time, annuals need lots of sun. Some annuals however are adapted to shade and will brighten lightly shaded or half-shaded spots with colorful flowers throughout the growing season.

The most popular annuals for planting in shady beds are impatiens (*Impatiens wallerana*), coleus (*Coleus x hybridus*), and begonias (*Begonia* species). So popular are these plants that they are nicknamed "the big three." There are many varieties of the big three to choose from; you'll find them listed in the charts on pages 30 to 34.

PERENNIALS

Flowering perennials are plants that live for many years in the garden and usually flower during a particular season—early spring or late summer for instance. They are herbaceous plants, meaning that the aboveground parts die to the ground during the winter, but the cold-hardy roots sprout new top growth each spring.

Flowering perennials don't require much care. They spread and the clumps increase in size, requiring dividing every several years.

You can replant the divisions and thus increase the number of plants you have.

Often the best perennials for shade gardens are hybrids of woodland plants such as columbine *(Aquilegia x hybrida)*, bellflowers *(Campanula* species), or foxglove *(Digitalis purpurea)*. These do well in both light shade and half shade and are most at home when planted in groups in a garden border. Wildflower species, such as trillium *(Trillium* species), bluebells *(Mertensia virginica)*, and violets *(Viola* species) look beautiful year after year planted in the shade of a grove of trees.

BULBS

Gardeners call plants that have fleshy underground storage parts "bulbs," though botanists distinguish bulbs further into "true bulbs," corms, rhizomes, and tubers. Bulbs usually bloom during or after a very active period of growth, then flowers and foliage die to the ground. The plant lies dormant for the rest of the year. In warm areas, some bulbs, such as Kaffir lily *(Clivia miniata)*, are evergreen.

Some bulbs grow and bloom in shade and others grow and bloom in sunny spots that become shaded later in the growing season. Early-blooming bulbs require sun from spring into early summer; their foliage naturally dies about the time late-leafing trees begin to cast heavy shade. Later-blooming bulbs will grow happily in light or half shade, where there is enough brightness for healthy growth and enough shade to prevent foliage from burning.

In mild climates, subtropical evergreen bulbs can be grown in light shade. They need protection from strong sun and from cold in winter.

To grow spring bulbs best, plant them in areas shaded by late-leafing deciduous trees such as sour gum *(Nyssa sylvatica)* or Amur cork tree *(Phellodendron amurense)*, or plant them beneath high-branching deciduous trees, such as some oaks

Hybrid tuberous begonias (*Begonia x tuberhybrida*) produce masses of blossoms in clear colors to brighten shady nooks from early spring through summer.

Bellflowers (*Campanula* sp.) create a delightful display when mass planted in a naturalistic setting in light shade.

Daffodils (*Narcissus* hybrids) bring the charm of their sunny blooms to shady garden sites during their spring flowering time.

A ferny dell tucked into a shady garden corner forms a cool retreat when the temperature is uncomfortable elsewhere in the yard.

Camellias (*Camellia* sp.) are attractive year round and are prized for their lavish flowers (shown below) that add garden color in winter months in mild climates.

(*Quercus* species), that form thick, broken canopies.

Crocus (*Crocus* species and hybrids) and daffodils (*Narcissus* hybrids) are very successful planted with evergreen ground-cover plants such as English ivy (*Hedera helix*), pachysandra (*Pachysandra terminalis*), or periwinkle (*Vinca minor*) in the shade beneath deciduous trees. They will add color to these ground covers during the spring season and the ground cover camouflages the withering foliage.

Later-blooming woodland bulbs such as the many species of *Scilla* will spread and naturalize in shady spots. When planted in masses, their display is truly breathtaking and they will persist and increase for many years.

FERNS

Most ferns are native to cool, moist, shaded forests or woodlands and are ideal plants for shady gardens. A special, indefinable beauty sets them apart from all other plants. They have delicate-looking foliage and a clumping habit that combines well with perennials and wildflowers.

Plant them in scattered groups in a woodland for a natural appearance or use them in a perennial border or in a shady side yard. A garden stream—even a tiny birdbath-sized pool—bordered with mossy rocks and a few ferns creates a charming focal point that makes a sanctuary of any shade garden. You can use tall ferns in clumps for bold effects, small ferns under shrubs, in planters, or in the crevices of shaded rock walls. Many ferns make excellent ground covers.

Ferns, in their amazing diversity, are widely used in shade gardens in every part of the continent. Ranging from 1 foot to 30 feet tall, ferns offer a broad choice. In form and texture, foliage is quite diverse—including the delicate tracery of rounded leaflets set on black wire-like stems of the maidenhair ferns (*Adiantum* species); the frilly fronds of mother fern (*Asplenium bulbiferum*), the massive finely-divided fronds of the palm-treelike tree ferns (several species); and the curiously downy, handlike fronds of staghorn fern (*Platycerium bifurcatum*).

Some ferns, like lady (*Athyrium filix-femina*), cinnamon (*Osmunda cinnamomea*), and giant chain ferns (*Woodwardia fimbriata*), adapt to boggy soils. At the other extreme, such ferns as bear's foot (*Humata tyermannii*), lace (*Microlepia strigosa*), and sword ferns (*Nephrolepis exaltata*) tolerate some dryness.

Most of the top-rated ferns are native North American plants. They are available at nurseries as container-grown plants and as bare-root plants from mail-order nurseries. It's best not to transplant ferns from the wild since some species are becoming endangered.

SHRUBS

Shrubs are the solid citizens of the garden. Bulbs, annuals, ferns, and perennials fill low spaces with color and greenery, but many of them come and go seasonally. Shrubs are the year-round mainstays of your shade garden, providing a backdrop for seasonal plants and often putting on a colorful show of flowers or fall foliage of their own. For shaded gardens, there is a wide and diverse choice of shrubs.

You may select deciduous shrubs, which drop their leaves for the winter, or evergreen ones, which retain their leaves year round. Semi-evergreen shrubs lose most of their leaves in cold climates and retain more of them where winters are milder.

The "big three" of flowering shrubs for shade are azaleas, rhododendrons, and camellias. They flower profusely in light or half shade and are handsome plants when not in bloom. Where they are adapted, these three groups of shrubs are unparalleled for their dependable performances.

Various types of azaleas are adapted to climates from Ontario to Florida, however the prime growing areas are mainly the states along the Atlantic Seaboard, coastal British Columbia, and the Northwest, where the climate is moist and the soil is acid. Evergreen azaleas are best adapted to the Southeast and the coastal areas of the West from central California to British Columbia, but hardier strains for colder areas have been developed. Deciduous azaleas thrive from Canada to the southern Appalachians and in the Northwest. Rhododendrons reach their pinnacle of perfection in the Northwest, but also thrive on the Atlantic Seaboard except in the hottest-summer areas of the South. All are worth the special care needed to grow them well outside their prime areas.

Camellias bloom in southern gardens (Zones 8 to 10) in fall and winter, when most other colors have been erased from the garden. Their waxy-petaled flowers and glossy leaves can be cut and enjoyed in vases and as corsages. Camellias combine well in lightly shaded gardens with azaleas and rhododendrons and in cold climates can be used as container plants on an enclosed, unheated porch or in a cool greenhouse.

VINES

Vines are problem solvers in many landscape situations and are invaluable in shady gardens. Taking up little ground space, a climbing vine is an ornamental asset in narrow gardens and side yards, which are usually shady most of the day. They can fill in the side of a narrow passageway without blocking it, covering the wall with year-round greenery or brilliant autumn color and winter tracery.

Climbing by clinging tendrils, twining stems, or adhesive discs, vines can quickly cover a blank wall or fence with softening foliage and flowers. Use them on a trellis or arbor to create privacy or act as a garden divider. Some shade-loving vines flower extravagantly and sometimes fragrantly; most make quick, solid ground covers even on steep banks and can cover open fences and arbors to provide shade and privacy.

Vines may be deciduous or evergreen, so choose the right kind according to the needs of your landscape. Perhaps year-round greenery is important, or maybe foliage in summer and openness in winter is desirable, if the vine is to cover a garden structure.

Vines, even more than other plants, grow vigorously and cover rapidly. Choose a fast grower, but remember that some fast growers don't stop where you want them to, or they mat heavily and require frequent thinning. Learn as much as you can about how a vine behaves before you buy and plant it.'

Many of the vines included in the chart on pages 50-52 are useful for growing on an overhead structure for the purpose of *creating* shade. Far faster-growing than trees, vines such as evergreen clematis *(Clematis armandii),* the jasmines *(Jasminum* species) and wisteria *(Wisteria* species) can cover pergolas, arbors, and open fences. But like other plants discussed in this book, these and other vines also grow in some degree of shade.

GROUND COVERS

Low plants that spread quickly by underground or trailing stems are called ground covers. They are admired for their ability to blanket the ground with foliage, and sometimes flowers, without needing much care. Ground covers can really dress up a garden, filling in spaces between other plants, creating an edging or border for a walkway, and growing in difficult shady or sunny sites. They are also useful for erosion control.

There are many beautiful ground covers suitable for creating low-maintenance plantings in shade gardens. The "big three" ground covers for shade are English ivy *(Hedera helix),* periwinkle *(Vinca minor),* and pachysandra *(Pachysandra terminalis).* These popular and easy-to-grow evergreen plants adapt to any kind of shade and are real problem solvers in deep shade, such as beneath the spreading branches of a beech tree *(Fagus* species), where it's difficult to grow anything.

Wisteria vines (*Wisteria* sp.) bear graceful trusses of flowers and create shade by clambering over trellises, pergolas, and arbors.

Pachysandra (*Pachysandra terminalis*) forms a dense ground cover in any kind of shade.

Japanese maple (*Acer palmatum*) casts light shade and is an excellent patio tree.

Maidenhair tree (*Ginkgo biloba*) is a well-behaved tree that is easy to garden under.

LAWNS

Most lawn grasses love sun, and the areas of the lawn shaded by trees or in narrow side yards are often thin and meager at best. This problem is usually due to planting the wrong kind of grass in the shady site. Several kinds of grass do well in light or half shade and can be planted either straight or as mixtures to create that desirable emerald-green sweep of lawn.

A mix for a shady lawn contains grasses adapted to various degrees of shade, so that coverage is complete. Usually the best-adapted grass will take over and crowd out the less successful varieties in each area. The chart on page 58 lists the best shade-tolerant grass varieties. Where shade is too deep even for these grasses, choose a ground cover such as English ivy (*Hedera helix*) or pachysandra (*Pachysandra terminalis*).

TREES

Trees are the visually dominant and most permanent plants in your yard and garden. *Canopy trees* are the tall trees that form a lofty ceiling, casting shade that determines what can—and can't—grow beneath them. Lower-growing, small trees that thrive in the shade of taller trees are called *understory trees*. Shade gardens often consist of tall canopy trees that are pruned high to accommodate a scattering of flowering understory trees beneath. Unless understory trees are planted too densely, they are usually open enough to plant shade-loving perennials, ferns, and ground covers beneath them.

The best trees for gardening beneath are high-branching, open ones that filter rather than block sunlight. They should have deep roots rather than surface-matting ones, so they don't compete with garden plants for moisture and nutrients. (Top-rated canopy trees are listed on page 11, understory trees are on pages 59-62.). Most of the recommended understory trees are North American woodland natives.

Because deciduous trees admit winter and early spring sunlight and, therefore, create more gardening possibilities, deciduous trees are preferred to evergreen ones in shade gardens. In addition to providing shade, many small trees bear beautiful flowers. Shadbush (*Amelanchier canadensis*), Eastern redbud (*Cercis canadensis*), flowering dogwood (*Cornus florida*), Cornelian cherry (*Cornus mas*), Japanese snowbell (*Styrax japonicus*), and hawthorns (*Crataegus* species) are among the early spring bloomers. Later bloomers are fringe tree (*Chionanthus virginicus*), sweet bay magnolia (*Magnolia virginiana*), and sourwood (*Oxydendrum arboreum*). For fall and winter color strawberry tree (*Arbutus unedo*) provides a spectacular flower show.

Many of these trees have colorful berries or interesting pods. Dogwoods (*Cornus* species), hollies (*Ilex* species), strawberry tree (*Arbutus unedo*), sourwood (*Oxydendrum arboreum*), hawthorns (*Crataegus* species), New Zealand laurel (*Corynocarpus laevigata*), Cornelian cherry (*Cornus mas*), and shadbush (*Amelanchier canadensis*) all offer visual excitement over extended periods of time. Japanese maples (*Acer palmatum*) and vine maples (*Acer circinatum*) bear winged seed capsules into autumn.

Colored foliage is another asset of many of these small trees. Some Japanese maple varieties are red throughout the season, and all are brilliant in fall. Leaves of Allegheny serviceberry (*Amelanchier laevis*) start and end the season colorfully.

The following trees are too shallow-rooted or cast too heavy a shade to garden under successfully: Norway maple (*Acer platanoides*), silver maple (*Acer saccharinum*), tree-of-heaven (*Ailanthus altissima*), modesto ash (*Fraxinus velutina*), walnut trees (*Juglans* species), southern magnolia (*Magnolia grandiflora*), poplar trees (*Populus* species).

Deciduous Trees for Casting Shade

Botanical/Common Name	Zones and Regions	Height/Spread	Comments
TREES THAT CAST LIGHT SHADE			
Albizia julibrissin — Silk Tree	7-10 A,B,C,D E,H,I,J	To 25-35 ft. high wider than tall.	Large leaves are divided into feathery leaflets. Pink, powder-pufflike blossoms held high above foliage in summer, followed by large seed pods. Heat and drought tolerant. Fast growing.
Acer palmatum — Japanese Maple	6-8 A,B,C, F,G,H,I	To 20-25 ft. high equally as wide.	A handsome small tree with lobed leaves that turn bright colors in fall. Well-behaved, excellent around patios. Many varieties available differing in size, leaf shape, and fall color. Some grow best in sun, others in partial shade.
Cladrastis lutea — Yellowwood	4-9 A,B,F, G,H,I	To 30 ft. high, 15 ft. wide.	One-foot-long compound leaves are divided into 7 to 11 leaflets. Foliage turns yellow in fall. Fragrant white flowers in long clusters bloom in spring. Good lawn tree. Tolerates wet soil.
Gleditsia triacanthos inermis 'Moraine' — Moraine Thornless Honey Locust	4-10 A-I	To 50 ft. high, 30 ft. wide.	Twice compound leaves divided into 7 to 15 leaflets. A good lawn tree. Tolerates wet soils.
Koelreuteria paniculata — Golden-Rain Tree	5-9 All regions.	To 30 ft. high, equally as wide.	1-1/2-foot-long compound leaves divided into 8 to 18 leaflets. Yellow flowers bloom in summer and are followed by interesting seedpods.
Phellodendron amurense — Amur Cork Tree	4-8 A,B,E, F,G,H,I	To 40 ft. high, equally as wide.	Leaves are 12 to 16 inches long and divided into 5 to 13 leaflets. A good lawn tree for cities and open areas.
TREES THAT CAST HALF SHADE			
Celtis occidentalis — Common Hackberry	4-8 A-I	To 40 ft. high, equally as wide.	Bright green leaves with toothed edges. Leafs-out late in spring. Good street tree. Tolerates drought and harsh conditions.
Cercidiphyllum japonicum — Katsura Tree	4-9 A,B,F, G,H,I,J	To 40 ft. high 20-30 ft. wide.	Leaves heart-shaped, 4 in. long, reddish when expanding in spring, gold and scarlet in fall. Protect from hot, drying wind.
Fraxinus species — Ash	2-10 All regions.	To 35-70 ft. high, and nearly as wide.	A large family of tough, fast-growing trees with leaves divided into as many as 12 to 13 leaflets. Tree size varies by species. Many have brightly colored fall foliage.
Ginkgo biloba — Maidenhair Tree	4-9 A,B,C, F,G,H,I	To 60 ft. high, equally as wide.	Leaves are fan-shaped, 4 inches wide, turn gold in autumn, drop all at once. A good lawn or street tree. Tolerates air pollution.
Nyssa sylvatica — Sour Gum	5-9 A,B,C,E, G,H,I,J	To 40 ft. high, 20 ft. wide.	Leaves are 2 to 6 inches long, turn brilliant orange-red in fall. Good lawn tree. Tolerates wet soil.
Pistacia chinensis — Chinese Pistache	7-10 B,C,D, E,I,J	To 60 ft. high, equally as wide.	Leaves are up to 12 inches long, divided into 10 to 16 leaflets, and turn bright yellow to fiery red in fall. Needs careful pruning when young.
TREES THAT CAST FULL SHADE			
Alnus species — Alders	3-10 A,B,C,E, F,G,H,I	To 35-90 ft. high, about half as wide.	Several species of fast-growing trees that thrive in wet soils. Useful where shade is needed quickly, but must be deep watered or will produce surface roots.
Morus alba — White Mulberry	5-9 All regions.	To 40 ft. high, 40-60 ft. wide.	An extremely fast growing tree valuable where shade is needed immediately. Tolerates extreme conditions, including heat and drought. Large lobed leaves turn yellow in fall. Choose fruitless varieties.
Platanus x acerifolia — London Plane Tree	5-10 A,B,C,D, E,G,H,I,J	To 50 ft. high, 30-40 ft. wide.	Leaves have 3 to 5 lobes and are 4 to 8 inches across. Good street or lawn tree. Fast growing. Tolerates drought, pollution, and wet soils.
Quercus coccinea — Scarlet Oak	4-9 All regions.	To 70 ft. high, 40-50 ft. wide.	Leaves have 7 to 9 deep lobes, 5 to 6 inches long, and turn scarlet in fall. Good street or lawn tree.
Quercus robur — English Oak	5-9 A,B,C, E,G,H,I	To 40-80 ft. high, equally as wide.	Leaves are 5 inches long with 3 to 7 rounded lobes. No fall color.
Quercus rubra — Northern Red Oak	4-10 A,B,C,E, F,G,H,I	To 60-80 ft. high, nearly as wide.	Leaves are 7 inches long with 7 to 11 lobes, turn red in fall. Native to the Eastern United States. Many other native American oaks make excellent shade trees.
Tilia cordata — Littleleaf Linden	4-8 A,B,E, F,G,H,I	To 40 ft. high, 20 ft. wide.	Heart-shaped leaves are 2-1/2 in. long, dark green with silvery undersides. Other species of linden also make good shade trees.

Designing Shade Gardens

A shade garden is not an entity unto itself. It can be a garden in just about any style you want it to be and differs from "sun gardens" only because the plants that grow there and the care techniques needed are different. Depending upon the type of shade you have, you can plant a traditional perennial flower border, a wildflower garden, a shrubbery border, or a landscaped garden retreat. Shade gardens can be as diverse in style and design as the gardeners planting them.

Perhaps the only common thread through all shade gardens is the lack of direct sunlight—this means that the garden site is naturally dim and must rely more heavily on the design of the garden to bring it out of obscurity. Understanding how to combine foliage and flowers to play up their interesting textures and how to use color to brighten a shaded area is basic to creating a shade garden that is as pleasing to look at as it is for the plants to grow in. Incorporating accents and focal points will help create a harmonious setting.

TEXTURE

Small finely divided leaves and dainty flowers have a *fine texture*, which is restful to look at and can be used effectively in large-scale plantings. On the other hand, plants with large, undivided leaves and big flowers have a *bold texture*. Bold textures are busier and more visually exciting than fine textures and should be used more sparingly than fine textures.

At left: By selecting plants carefully, your shade garden can include colorful flowers all during the year.

Aaron's beard (*Hypericum calycinum*)

Boston ivy (*Parthenocissus* sp.)

Camellia (*Camellia* sp.)

Peony (*Paeonia* hybrid)

A ground cover planting of fine-textured periwinkle (*Vinca minor*) is a beautiful foil for the picturesque drama of a rugged tree trunk.

To keep a shade garden filled with visual excitement, arrange blooming plants, such as these tulips (*Tulipa* sp.) in a mass.

Siberian scilla (*Scilla siberica*) naturalizes freely in shady sites, offering its rich blue, bell-shaped flowers in early summer.

In a shade garden, where the light is already somewhat dim, the shadows cast by bold-leaved plants are larger and darker than those of small-leaved plants. This is something to consider when you are trying to brighten up an area. Overusing tall large-leaved plants will further cast the area into darkness. Fine-textured plants that filter but do not stop the light will keep it brighter.

You will notice too that fine-textured plants seem smaller and farther away than they really are. And just the opposite seems true of bold-textured plants. A rule of thumb followed by many gardeners is that in small enclosed gardens fine-textured plants should predominate and the bold-textured ones are best planted in small clumps as accents; in larger, more open gardens, bold-textured plants can be used in larger sweeps in the distant areas, with the closer plants becoming increasingly more fine-textured. This gradation in texture creates a visually harmonious arrangement of plants.

To create interesting textural patterns, contrast bold- and fine-textured foliage plants. It is usually best to plant the finer-textured ones in a large group and contrast this with a smaller clump of bold-textured foliage. For instance, in a ground cover planting of the small-leaved periwinkle *(Vinca minor)*, you might plant several clumps of plantain lily *(Hosta* species)—its clusters of broad upright leaves are effectively set off by the small ovals of the periwinkle, creating an accent that draws your eye. Without the contrasting bold-textured foliage, the periwinkle would look pretty but have no focus. If the same area were planted with a mass of plantain lily, the many big leaves would become a busy clutter of overpowering foliage.

Plan too for interesting winter textures, visualizing how your shade garden will appear when deciduous plants are bare. Bare stems of even bold-leaved plants often take on a fine-texture, especially if the shrubs are very twiggy.

COLOR

Yellows, reds, and oranges are warm colors that suggest sunlight and heat. Blues, greens, and purples are cool colors that seem to make the temperature drop a few degrees. In a shade garden, you may choose to use warm colors in a perennial border, for instance, if you wish to down play the shade. But in a woodland setting where you wish to reinforce the image of cooling shade, planting flowers of blue and lavender work to your advantage.

The most important aspect of choosing flower and foliage colors for shady spots is to consider whether the colors reflect light or absorb it. Shadows tend to absorb color, but bright color or massed color shines through. For instance, white and pale pastels are bright colors and will bounce light back into the garden. But deep purple and red are dark colors that absorb light and will recede further into the shadows. A large sweep of white-flowered impatiens planted beneath a tree will make the area glow, however, if the same area were planted instead with red-flowered impatiens, the area would seem dimmer still.

You can use combinations of colors to create effective displays. A favorite for shade gardens is a combination of blue and white flowers, which are very cooling together with green foliage. Other themes might be pink and lavender, or yellow, blue, and white. When dark colors are used, use them sparingly in contrast to the brighter, lighter shades.

Green gardens: Many shade gardens are predominately foliage gardens. There's nothing wrong with that, but their beauty depends even more upon the contrast of textures, arrangement of plants, and incorporation of pleasing accents. It is important that you plan carefully to achieve the effect you are striving for. Calm green gardens can play up the contrast of the many shades of green. Use the steel-blue green of bold-textured blue-leafed plantain lily *(Hosta sieboldiana)* to set off the delicate emerald-green foliage of maidenhair fern *(Adiantum pedatum)*. As a taller backdrop for the two plants, use the dark green needled foliage of yew *(Taxus baccata)*. Amongst these plants, you can set a stone container of pink- and-white-leaved caladiums *(Caladium* hybrids), to add an element of striking contrast which will act as a bright focal point.

Color all year: Most plants have a season or two when they are colorful and the rest of the year they are quietly green or brown. A well-planned garden changes with the seasons, but has color in it year round—you can choose annuals for color all summer, perennials and flowering shrubs for color during particular seasons, and shrubs and trees with bright berries or mottled and colored bark to add interest in winter. And don't forget those all-important evergreen plants whose greenery is welcome throughout the year.

Many flowering shrubs, kurume azaleas *(Rhododendron* hybrids) for example, make sheets of color when in bloom and provide greenery for the balance of the year. The reddish autumn foliage and scarlet berries of heavenly bamboo *(Nandina domestica)* brighten the shaded garden in fall and winter. Variegated forms of *Hosta* light up shaded spots with white-bordered leaves. The vivid red stems of red-twig dogwood *(Cornus stolonifera)* and the green stems of Japanese kerria *(Kerria japonica)* enliven the winter landscape and are especially handsome when dusted with new fallen snow.

FOCAL POINTS

Every garden is more attractive if there is one spot that draws the eye and acts as a focal point. This may be the most colorful plant in an area, the tallest one, or some inanimate object such as a birdbath or statue. If the focal point is a plant, it may change with the seasons—as

Every garden setting is more appealing if there is a focal point such as is provided here by the thornless honey locust tree (*Gleditisia triacanthos inermis* 'Moraine').

Evergreen azaleas (*Rhododendron* sp.) are shade-loving shrubs that make a handsome informal border.

Canadian hemlocks (*Tsuga canadensis*) can be pruned to make an excellent evergreen screen or hedge in shady spots.

A refreshing woodland effect results when azaleas and rhododendrons (*Rhododendron* sp.) are naturalized under tall trees that let light filter through.

one shrub goes out of bloom, your eye may be drawn to another part of the garden where a different shrub is displaying its blossoms.

When arranging the plants in your shade garden, consider what will be the focal points, then design the planting to emphasize them visually. For instance, locating a bird bath in the narrowest part of a curving flower bed makes it seem top-heavy, but placing it in the widest part visually anchors it in the expanse of flowers and foliage. A shrub border is most effectively designed with the tallest shrub positioned about a third of the way from the far end of the bed, with the heights of the other shrubs in the border diminishing in either direction.

SHRUBS IN SHADE GARDENS

Growing at a height intermediate between the ceiling of trees and the carpet of low-growing plants, many shrubs are seen at, or close to, eye level. Whether used as a hedge, screen, accent, background, or foundation planting, shrubs figure strongly in garden design. They are permanent elements of your garden and should therefore be used thoughtfully.

Formal uses: Shaped shrubs are the dominant formal element of many gardens. Sheared hedges of boxwood (*Buxus* species), privet (*Ligustrum* species), and Canadian hemlock (*Tsuga canadensis*) are frequently used to establish garden outlines and property boundaries. Shrubs that are readily trained as espaliers on a wall or fence create a bold, striking formal effect but take up hardly any ground space.

Informal uses: Shrubs pruned to retain their natural shapes can provide substance, texture, and color in a woodland-style garden, an informal shrub border, or a free-form hedge: rhododendrons (*Rhododendron* hybrids), deciduous or evergreen azaleas (*Rhododendron* species and hybrids) and red-twig dogwood (*Cornus stolonifera*) are among many choice woodland shrubs.

SHADE PLANTS IN CONTAINERS

Shady spots are easily and quickly brightened up with plants grown in containers. You can nestle a large planter of white-leaved caladiums (*Caladium* hybrids) in the English ivy (*Hedera helix*) beneath a wide-spreading tree, for instance, to create an eye-catching focal point. Most perennials and annuals make first-rate container plants. You can group or hang them, rearrange and move them as they go in and out of bloom, and change them to follow the seasonal shifting of the sun.

A tub or even a shallow pot of bulbs such as tulips (*Tulipa* hybrids) or daffodils (*Narcissus* hybrids) makes a brilliant accent for a shady spot. It's best after the bulb blossoms fade to move the container to an out-of-the-way sunny spot for the foliage to cure. Spring-blooming bulbs are best kept in planters for only one season. You can plant them in the garden in fall and replant the container with fresh bulbs, if you wish.

Shrubs and small trees can be grown in large tubs and planters and placed on paved areas where there is no open soil. Use them on the front porch on either side of the door to frame the entrance or as focal points on a terrace or patio.

MAKING PEOPLE WELCOME

In landscaped areas where people are meant to walk or sit, a garden set in shade can be a cool, beckoning retreat if it offers some welcome for people as well as for plants. A path leading through a bed of ferns and ivy to a bench beneath a tree can be a simple device that leads the eye and the viewer into the garden.

In woodland settings, paths of shredded bark or tree-trunk rounds have an attractive naturalistic appearance that blends in with the scene. Select wooden or stone benches for such a setting. In more formal gardens, choose brick or flagstone walkways and wrought-iron benches and tables. When the accessories you add to the garden are in keeping with the style of the garden, you create a sense of unity between the plants and their setting.

In deep shade, where the choice of plants is limited, you might consider covering large areas with bricks or flagstones to create a terrace and then using container-grown plants to soften the area and to add interest. This is a low-maintenance alternative that can dress up a garden and create a welcome feeling.

A pleasing addition to any style of shade garden is the sound of falling water. You might wish to create your own brook, complete with waterfall, but an easier way to provide the enjoyment and cooling effect of water in motion is to simply purchase a small bubbling fountain with a recirculating pump from your garden center.

PLANT COMBINATIONS

One of the great pleasures of gardening in the shade is formulating your own plant combinations. Garden designers generally feel that horticulturally compatible plants combine beautifully, no matter what their origin. So unless you are a purist, don't worry about planting North American native plants such as eastern redbud *(Cercis canadensis)* and flowering dogwood *(Cornus florida)* with Asian plants such as Korean dogwood *(Cornus kousa)* and Japanese maple *(Acer palmatum)*. These are adapted to similar environments, even though they are native to different parts of the world, and will look beautiful and grow beautifully together.

A combination often seen in shady gardens in the Southeast is masses of evergreen azaleas *(Rhododendron* hybrids) planted close to an understory of American holly *(Ilex opaca)*, high-pruned eastern redbud *(Cercis canadensis)*, and flowering dogwood *(Cornus florida)*. These are in turn shaded by the sparse-needled branches of tall pines *(Pinus* species), which admits brightness and constantly shifting shadows.

The controlled environment created by lath-screening in a plant room provides ideal growing conditions for a wide range of choice plants.

One of the most pleasing plant combinations seen in shade gardens is azaleas (*Rhododendron* sp.) backdropped by a Japanese maple (*Acer palmatum*).

Caring for Shade Gardens

At left: Shade-loving azaleas (*Rhododendron* sp.) require little care and are perfect for low-maintenance gardens.

Gardening in the shade is not quite the same as gardening in the sun. It is no more difficult—the challenge lies only in understanding the special conditions of a shady garden site—but success does depend upon close observation. Soil conditions are different, and water and fertilizer needs are not the same as in sunny areas. Shady, moist conditions may encourage fungus diseases that are rarely seen in sunny locations. The trees whose canopies provide shade plants with the proper light exposure and modify summer temperatures may also pose the problem of greedy tree roots that compete with smaller plants for moisture and nutrients.

Shade changes: Shade can also change subtly over the years without your noticing, so that it suddenly seems one summer to have become dramatically deeper. As trees grow and mature, their limbs reach out more and their trunks grow taller, casting shadows farther. Leaves may grow more thickly and shade is less open. What was once light shade may become more like deep shade, and half shade may turn into all-day shade.

If you observe how the shade changes each year, you can modify your gardening techniques and replant, if necessary, with better-suited plants. You may also wish to prune trees to keep them open and to prevent the shade from becoming too dark. The unexpected removal of a tree due to storm damage or disease can suddenly expose a shade garden to full

Fancy-leaved caladium (*Caladium x hortulanum*)

Knap Hill/Exbury azalea (*Rhododendron* hybrid)

Burford holly (*Ilex cornuta* 'Burfordii')

Japanese honeysuckle (*Lonicera* sp.)

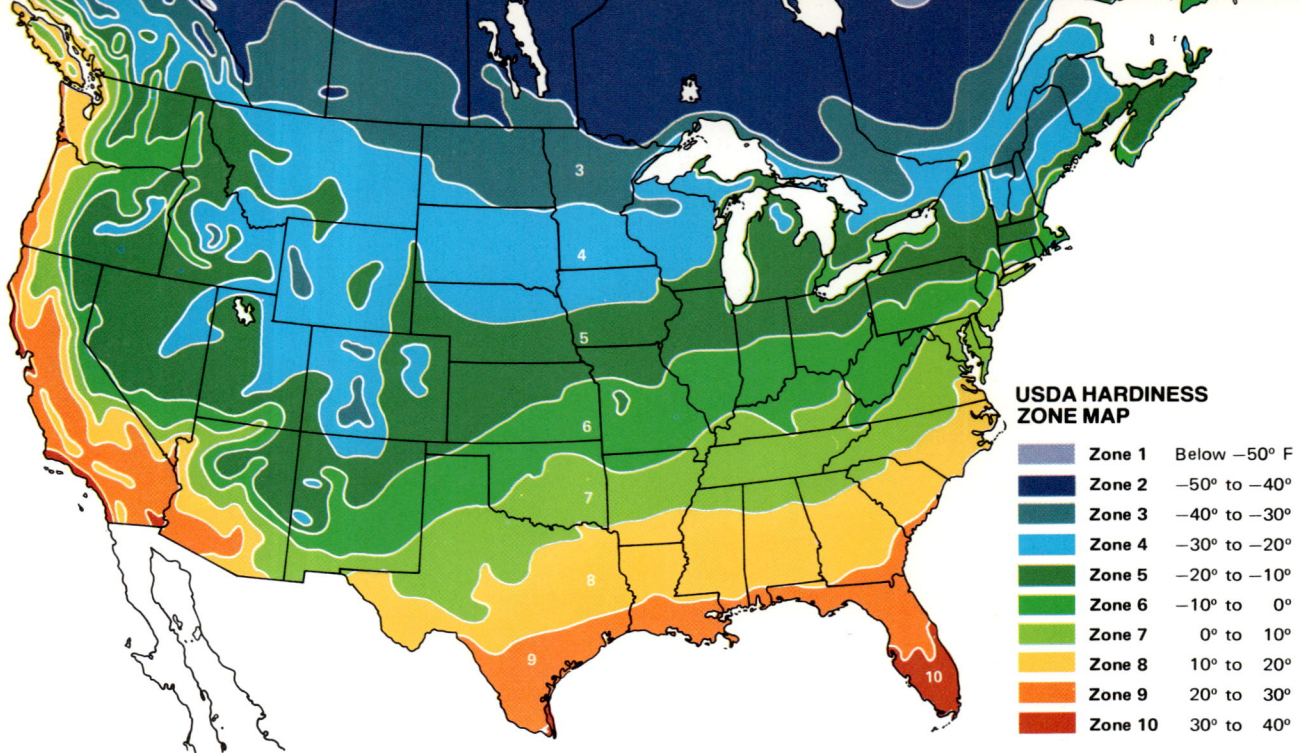

sun; this requires constructing a temporary sunscreen, if valuable flowering trees, shrubs, and perennials are to survive.

CLIMATE

The first step in having a successful shade garden is choosing appropriate plants that are suited to your climate. The USDA plant hardiness map shown above records the average low temperatures that occur throughout the United States and Southern Canada. It divides North America into 10 zones with the average minimum temperature of each zone differing by 10 degrees Fahrenheit. Since a plant's adaptation is often limited by the amount of winter cold it can tolerate, all plants described in this book are identified by the zones where they will give a top-rated performance. Use the map to find your hardiness zone so you can select appropriate plants for your garden.

As every gardener learns, cold hardiness is only one factor of a plant's adaptation. A plant's ability to do well in a certain location depends upon unique combinations of soil type, wind, rainfall, length and time of cold, humidity, summer temperatures, and temperatures in relation to humidity.

The USDA hardiness zone map does not take other climate factors into consideration. To give you additional help in choosing the best plants for your yard and garden, the plants are also identified by which regions of the country they are adapted to. The map on the next page separates the United States and Canada into 10 gardening regions based on climate trends. Find your climate region and then be sure that any plant you choose is recommended for both your USDA zone and your climate region.

Because gardening successfully in the shade depends upon understanding your garden's environment, more help is given here on climate trends. The chart on page 22 shows the percent of sunshine in July. This will help you understand just how much sun your plants are actually getting in the lightly shaded or half-shaded areas of your garden. Shade in the foggy coastal area of Oregon, for instance, is more intense than shade in the cities located in Missouri and Indiana. A plant that may need "full sun" in foggy San Francisco may need "light shade" in Fresno, when the percent of sunshine is taken into consideration.

Knowing the last frost dates in spring and the first frost dates in fall guide you in determining the proper planting times. Statistics for various cities in the United States are listed for last frost in spring, first frost in fall, percent of sunshine for June, July, August, and September, and maximum/minimum temperatures (°F) for the same months.

Obviously the shade beneath a deciduous tree will be different than the shade cast by an evergreen tree. Deciduous trees as a class are out of leaf for five months or more, including the early spring months when temperatures are high enough to encourage flowering of many bulbs and shrubs in the full sun beneath the tree's branches.

Since different tree species leaf out and drop their leaves at various times, the amount of shade beneath different trees can be quite variable. This can affect the vigor of the plants you grow beneath deciduous trees. For instance, early spring-flowering bulbs may do best when planted so as to receive maximum sunshine in spring; they are best planted beneath late-leafing trees. (See the chart on the next page.)

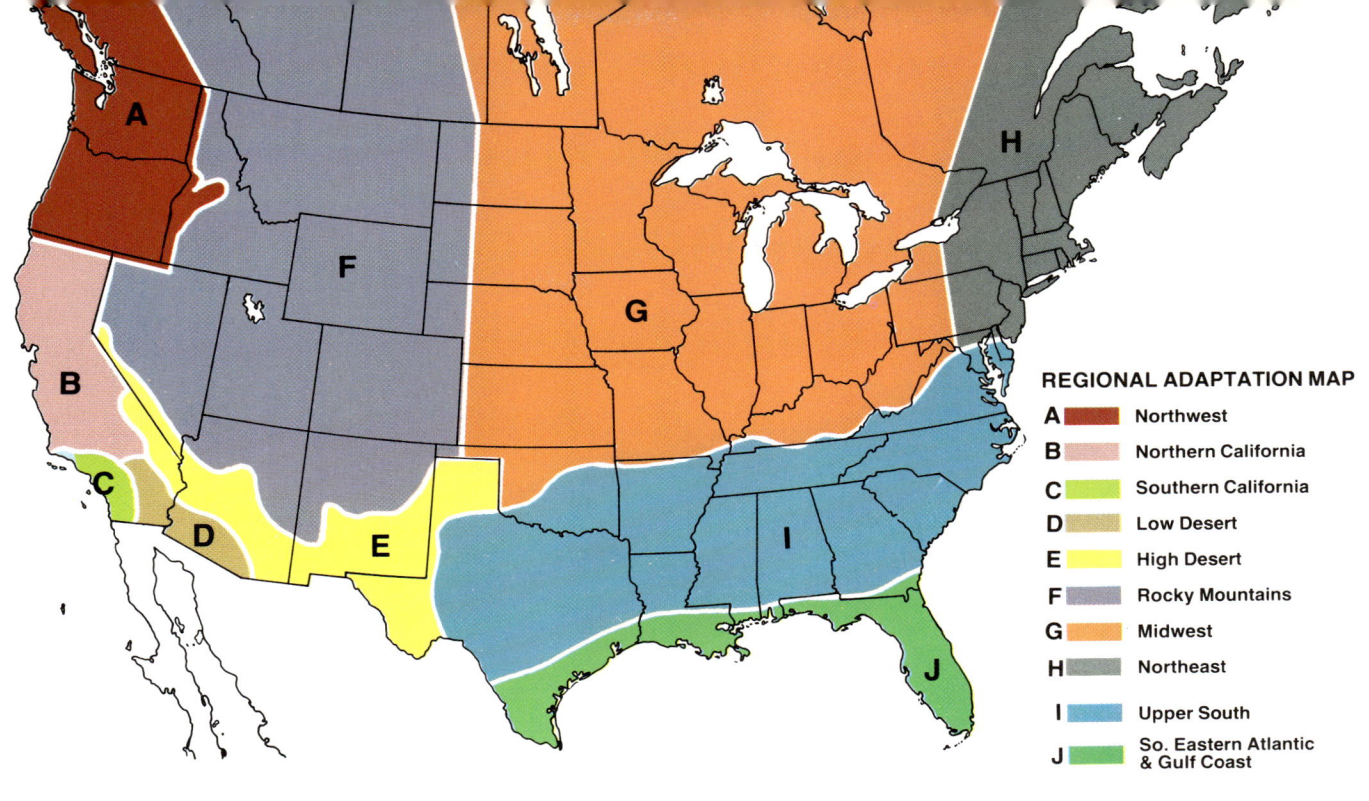

REGIONAL ADAPTATION MAP

- A Northwest
- B Northern California
- C Southern California
- D Low Desert
- E High Desert
- F Rocky Mountains
- G Midwest
- H Northeast
- I Upper South
- J So. Eastern Atlantic & Gulf Coast

Leaf-Fall and Leaf-Emergence Dates

The following chart lists the approximate times of leaf-fall and leaf-emergence in Aurora, Oregon, of some popular shade trees as recorded by the North Willamette Experiment Station.

Exact dates in your own area will be different of course, however, differences between each species will be the same number of weeks.

Species	Leaf Fall*	Leaf Emergence**
Carpinus betulus European Hornbeam	4th week November	2nd week April
Celtis occidentalis Common Hackberry	2nd week November	2nd week April
Cladrastis lutea American Yellowwood	1st week November	1st week April
Fraxinus pennsylvanica 'Marshall' Marshall Seedless Green Ash	3rd week October	1st week April
Ginkgo biloba (male) 'Fairmont' Fairmont Maidenhair Tree	3rd week November	4th week April
Koelreuteria paniculata Golden-Rain Tree	2nd week November	1st week April

Species	Leaf Fall*	Leaf Emergence**
Nyssa sylvatica Sour Gum	2nd week November	4th week April
Phellodendron amurense Amur Cork Tree	4th week October	4th week March
Platanus x acerifolia London Plane Tree	3rd week November	2nd week April
Quercus coccinea Scarlet Oak	4th week December	4th week April
Quercus robur English Oak	4th week December	4th week April
Quercus rubra Red Oak	1st week December	4th week April
Tilia cordata Little-Leaf Linden	2nd week November	4th week April

*Defoliation date is date of 100% defoliation.
**Leaf emergence is date when first leaves appear.

Climate Patterns of American Cities

The last spring frost and first fall frost dates, the percent of sunshine, and the maximum/minimum temperatures (°F) for June, July, August, and September are shown below for cities throughout the United States.

WEST COAST

City	June	July	Aug	Sept
Denver, CO	71%	71%	72%	75%
First fall frost: Oct 12	81°/53°F	86°/59°F	85°/58°F	77°/48°F
Last spring frost: May 5				
Fresno, CA	95%	96%	96%	95%
First fall frost: Nov 19	90°/57°F	98°/63°F	96°/61°F	91°/56°F
Last spring frost: Mar 14				
Portland, OR	44%	66%	58%	61%
First fall frost: Nov 24	79°/52°F	85°/53°F	89°/59°F	73°/52°F
Last spring frost: Mar 6				
Red Bluff, CA	89%	96%	94%	92%
First fall frost: Dec 5	89°/62°F	98°/67°F	96°/64°F	91°/60°F
Last spring frost: Mar 6				
Salt Lake City, UT	79%	84%	83%	84%
First fall frost: Nov 1	81°/55°F	91°/63°F	89°/62°F	78°/52°F
Last spring frost: Apr 12				
San Diego, CA	57%	68%	69%	68%
First fall frost: None	71°/60°F	75°/64°F	77°/65°F	76°/63°F
Last spring frost: None				
Seattle, WA	49%	63%	56%	53%
First fall frost: Nov 24	70°/52°F	76°/56°F	74°/55°F	69°/52°F
Last spring frost: Mar 14				
Tucson, AZ	93%	78%	82%	87%
First fall frost: Nov 24	99°/65°F	99°/73°F	97°/71°F	94°/66°F
Last spring frost: Mar 10				

MIDWEST

City	June	July	Aug	Sept
Evansville, IN	73%	76%	76%	70%
First fall frost: Nov 4	85°/64°F	89°/67°F	87°/65°F	82°/59°F
Last spring frost: Apr 2				
Indianapolis, IN	67%	70%	71%	66%
First fall frost: Oct 27	83°/60°F	88°/64°F	86°/62°F	79°/55°F
Last spring frost: Apr 17				
Kansas City, MO	69%	76%	73%	69%
First fall frost: Oct 30	85°/66°F	92°/71°F	90°/69°F	83°/60°F
Last spring frost: Apr 6				
St. Louis, MO	69%	71%	69%	64%
First fall frost: Nov 1	85°/63°F	89°/67°F	87°/66°F	81°/58°F
Last spring frost: Apr 9				
Springfield, MO	66%	70%	72%	71%
First fall frost: Oct 30	85°/63°F	90°/67°F	90°/66°F	83°/58°F
Last spring frost: Apr 12				

EAST COAST

City	June	July	Aug	Sept
Boston, MA	63%	66%	66%	64%
First fall frost: Nov. 7	76°/58°F	81°/64°F	79°/63°F	79°/61°F
Last spring frost: Apr 8				
Burlington, VT	60%	65%	61%	54%
First fall frost: Oct 3	78°/53°F	82°/58°F	80°/56°F	71°/48°F
Last spring frost: May 8				
Hartford, CT	60%	62%	60%	57%
First fall frost: Oct 19	81°/57°F	86°/62°F	83°/60°F	76°/52°F
Last spring frost: Apr 22				
New Haven, CT	64%	66%	64%	63%
First fall frost: Oct 27	75°/56°F	80°/62°F	79°/61°F	73°/54°F
Last spring frost: Apr 15				
Providence, RI	63%	63%	62%	60%
First fall frost: Oct 27	75°/56°F	80°/62°F	79°/60°F	72°/53°F
Last spring frost: Apr 13				
Washington D.C.	64%	63%	63%	62%
First fall frost: Nov. 10	84°/65°F	87°/69°F	86°/68°F	79°/61°F
Last spring frost: Mar 29				

SOUTH

City	June	July	Aug	Sept
Atlanta, GA	67%	62%	65%	63%
First fall frost: Nov 18	87°/66°F	88°/69°F	88°/68°F	83°/63°F
Last spring frost: Mar 21				
Houston, TX	66%	67%	63%	58%
First fall frost: Dec 11	90°/69°F	93°/71°F	92°/71°F	88°/68°F
Last spring frost: Feb 5				
Miami, FL	69%	74%	72%	68%
First fall frost: None	88°/74°F	89°/75°F	89°/76°F	88°/75°F
Last spring frost: None				
Montgomery, AL	66%	63%	66%	62%
First fall frost: Dec 3	90°/69°F	92°/72°F	92°/71°F	88°/66°F
Last spring frost: Feb 27				
New Orleans, LA	67%	57%	55%	60%
First fall frost: Dec 9	90°/71°F	91°/73°F	91°/73°F	87°/69°F
Last spring frost: Feb 20				
Savannah, GA	64%	63%	63%	58%
First fall frost: Nov 29	90°/69°F	91°/71°F	91°/71°F	86°/67°F
Last spring frost: Feb 27				
Shreveport, LA	70%	73%	71%	67%
First fall frost: Nov 15	91°/71°F	93°/73°F	94°/73°F	88°/67°F
Last spring frost: Mar 8				
Tampa, FL	66%	61%	59%	60%
First fall frost: None	89°/72°F	90°/74°F	90°/74°F	88°/73°F
Last spring frost: None				

SHADY MICROCLIMATES

Microclimates are the small climates around your home that differ slightly from the general climate of your area. For instance, the northern side of your house is usually in shadow most of the day. The lack of direct sun there makes the area colder than the southern side of your house, which receives sun all day unless it's shaded by trees.

The shady areas of your garden will of course be cooler than sunny areas of your property, however, you should study your shady garden spots carefully to see if they are influenced in other ways. If air circulation is poor because the prevailing winds are blocked by a building or a hedge, the spot may be unusually humid, inviting fungus diseases. If the spot is low-lying, it may be a frost pocket, because cold air flows and sinks to the lowest spot, much like running water. If a large area of pavement, which heats up from solar radiation, is nearby, the spot may be warmer than expected and could be too hot and dry for some sensitive shade plants.

Understanding how these microclimates modify your garden conditions will increase your success in your shade gardening endeavors. For instance, plants that are borderline hardy for your area may do well if you take protective measures such as providing wind or snow shelters and making use of your property's warm microclimates. Protected plants can often be grown successfully in the next colder zone.

You can create shady microclimates that will function well as shade garden sites by building an overhead shelter, or by a series of simple baffle panels. These cast shade and direct air currents and are easy to construct. They can be as inexpensive as the price of a piece of canvas, a short length of rope, and some 2×4s for framing.

Deciduous trees help conserve energy. In summer they provide cool shade for ornamental plants and for your house itself.

During winter deciduous trees let the sunlight through their bare branches, warming your house and lowering your heating costs.

SOIL FOR SHADE GARDENS

The soil on a forest floor is naturally moist, rich, and crumbly because it is composed of decomposed leaves, twigs, and other plant matter, which forms a natural rich compost. But frequently in home landcapes the soil beneath trees becomes hard and compacted because every autumn a major clean-up effort is carried out and not a fallen leaf is left to remain on the ground. This robs the soil of its natural method of renewal and it becomes depleted of nutrients and inhospitable for gardening.

Beneath a stand of trees, it is advisable not to rake up fallen leaves each autumn. This area is suitable for planting a woodland garden and the fallen leaves will not look unsightly if the area is landscaped with informally grouped shrubs, ferns, and perennials. (Be sure however to remove fallen leaves, if they dropped due to fungus diseases.) If you find the fallen leaves objectionable, then by all means rake them up, but keep the soil covered with a deep mulch. (See mulching on this page.)

Planting in compacted soil: When planting an area of compacted soil for the first time, loosen it up by the gentle use of a garden fork. Spread an inch or two of organic matter across the top of the loosened soil and then hoe it in. Water slowly and deeply with a sprinkler. You are ready to plant in a day or two when the soil has dried slightly.

In areas where thick tree roots are exposed and small roots form a dense mat, you may have difficulty loosening the soil. If this is the case, you can dig out pockets of compacted soil with a garden spade and replace the old soil with enriched soil. Plant ground covers, ferns, or perennials in these pockets of improved soil, where they will get quickly established.

WATERING SHADE GARDENS

Most shade-loving plants are also moisture-loving plants. However, there are no hard-and-fast rules to go by when it comes to watering shade gardens. The key to success is close observation, since each shady site is an individual case.

More often than not, the soil in a shaded site is moist and remains moist for some time after a rain or a watering, because the shaded area is cool. Half-shaded areas, especially those that receive afternoon sun, will be warmer and will dry faster. But beneath the overhang of a house or beneath a densely foliaged tree, rain may be deflected and the shady spot may actually be unusually dry.

Surface tree roots can also quickly rob the topsoil of moisture. Deep-rooted trees do not pose this problem, but surface-rooted ones are difficult to garden under. Where surface-rooted trees are a problem, it helps to water the area deeply and thoroughly, allowing a sprinkler to run gently all day, several times a month during the growing season. This will encourage the roots to grow deeper in search of water. Watering so that only the top several inches of soil is wetted only makes the problem worse. Newly planted trees should be deeply watered to encourage deep roots.

When watering shade plants, it is best to water in early morning so that the plants can dry off before nightfall—this discourages fungus diseases. If possible, drip irrigation systems or hoses that allow water to seep slowly into the soil without wetting foliage is preferable to overhead sprinklers.

How often you should water depends upon how quickly the soil dries. And that in turn depends upon many factors such as the temperature, soil type, and kinds of trees and smaller plants growing in the garden. Most garden plants do best with the equivalent of an inch of rain a week during the growing season. If rain doesn't help you out, then you'll have to supply water when the top inch of soil seems dry. If the soil dries very rapidly, then you aren't supplying enough water for both the tree roots and your garden plants.

FERTILIZER NEEDS IN SHADE GARDENS

Plants growing in the shade cast by trees will need special attention when it comes to fertilizing. Apply a balanced fertilizer, such as 5-10-5 (5% nitrogen, 10% phosphorus, and 5% potassium) several times during the growing season, at the rate recommended for trees. The trees will get most of the nutrients, leaving a modest supply for your other plants.

It's best to apply fertilizer in early spring just before growth begins, and then once a month until midsummer. By the end of summer, plants should be slowing down to prepare for winter dormancy—fertilizing at that time will encourage new growth that may be damaged by fall frosts.

Shade gardens that are shaded by buildings rather than trees will need less fertilizer. Apply fertilizer at the rate recommended for the particular plants you are feeding.

Azaleas, rhododendrons, camellias, and hollies are shade-loving plants that require acid soil. When fertilizing them, it is important to choose a fertilizer that is designed for acid-loving plants. Such a plant food contains its nutrients in chemical forms that these plants can readily absorb.

MULCHING SHADE GARDENS

Mulch is a layer of material spread across the surface of the soil. It may be organic or inorganic and acts to conserve moisture, shade out weeds, and improve the appearance of the garden. An organic mulch, such as shredded bark, sawdust, pine needles, and compost, improves the fertility and texture of the soil as it decomposes. Inorganic mulches, such as pebbles, stones, and gravel, do not improve the soil but are ornamental in certain garden situations and do not need replacing as frequently as do organic mulches.

Shade gardens, like sun gardens, benefit from being mulched. The mulch will help keep roots cool and the soil moist, conditions preferred by most shade plants. Spread mulch about two inches deep over the soil in the planting bed. Add fresh mulch each spring, if needed. In areas with cold winters, an extra application of mulch heaped around borderline hardy plants after the soil freezes in fall will help them survive the winter.

As organic mulches decay, they use nitrogen from the soil. Be sure that you fertilize mulched plants well so they do not suffer from nitrogen deficiency. Rake back the mulch and spread the fertilizer directly on the soil.

Watering

Apply water slowly so that it soaks through mulch and into soil without runoff.

Several kinds of sprinklers work efficiently and are a convenient way to apply water. The spray washes and cools leaves.

A soaker hose applies water efficiently at a rate soil can absorb, directly over rootball.

Mulching

A 2- to 3-inch layer of non-compressing pine needles is a long-lasting, attractive, acid mulch.

Fallen leaves make a good mulch. The mulch layer should be deeper than other mulches as leaves pack down when wet.

A mulch of fir bark is long-lasting and attractive. It is widely available and helps maintain proper pH and moisture.

Fertilizing and Special Care

Granular fertilizer is most beneficial when applied directly on top of soil under mulch.

Bury long-lasting fertilizer pellets, 2 or 3 inches below soil and beyond the outer edges of the rootball.

Hosing plants with plain or soapy water helps prevent and control problem pests such as aphids.

Pruning Shrubs and Trees in the Shade Garden

A shrub will lose vigor and become susceptible to disease if it becomes too dense and overgrown.

Improve air circulation and rejuvenate deciduous shrubs by cutting out the oldest stems at ground level, after blooming in spring.

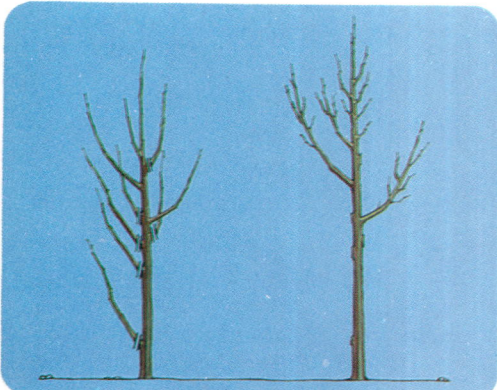

Let in more light by thinning trees to curtail development of new shoots and direct growth. Thinning cuts to be made, shown at left. Resulting growth, shown at right.

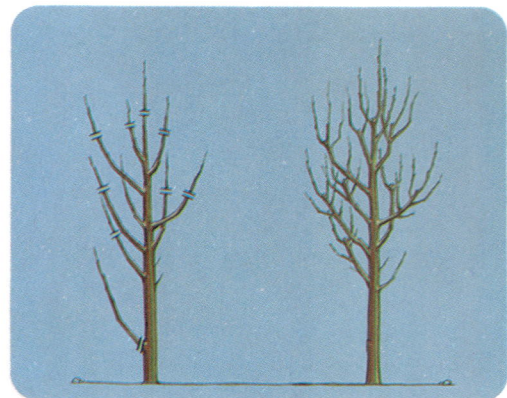

Create denser shade by heading a tree to increase the production of new shoots and stiffen main branches. Heading cuts to be made, shown at left. Resulting growth, shown at right.

Make pruning cuts above an outward-facing bud to direct new growth outward.

To remove heavy limb (left): 1) undercut, 2) cut through limb, 3) remove stub. To remove dead stub (right): Cut flush with healthy growth, not trunk.

AIR CIRCULATION

Since shaded gardens are often cool and damp, the plants in them are sometimes subject to fungus diseases, which thrive in just such conditions. (See Pests and Problems on page 27.) Improving air circulation will help dry the plants and discourage disease.

One way to ensure good air circulation is to avoid planting shrubs and small trees too closely. Proper spacing that allows air movement between plants is important, especially in muggy climates. Most people tend to plant new plants close together because they are small, but as the plants mature they often crowd each other. If this is the case in your garden, do not hesitate to remove overcrowded shrubs—they can be transplanted elsewhere in the garden if you wish.

Side yards may be either open to the prevailing breezes or protected from them depending upon the location of buildings and fences. If air is stagnant in narrow yards, then open them up, if you can, by removing solid fences and replacing them with lattice-work or some other open style that allows air to pass. Tall hedges and shrubbery may also be blocking the breeze and can be removed or pruned to encourage air movement.

LETTING IN MORE LIGHT

Where shade is too dark to grow the kind of shade garden you want, you don't have to resign yourself to the situation. You can bring in more light where thickly foliaged trees and even the shadow of a building are too dark.

Since most excessive shade results from dense overgrown trees and large shrubs, pruning or occasionally removal often work miraculous transformations. Prune trees high, removing lower limbs, so their branches are far enough above the ground to diffuse rather than block light. In the tree's crown, remove selected branches by *thinning*, a pruning method in which entire main or side branches are removed at their origins. This kind of pruning will allow more light to filter through the tree, brightening the area underneath. If trees are too closely planted to admit light, remove some and thin the remaining ones.

Where excessive shade results from the shadows of buildings, you may think it's an impossible situation to solve. However, there are ways to brighten open shaded areas. The shaded wall or fence, as well as any nearby wall or fence that catches and reflects sunlight, should be painted white or a pastel color. Changing the paint from a dark to a light color can instantly transform a gloomy area suited only to moss and mushrooms into a much brighter spot that fills with reflected light and encourages many beautiful shade-loving plants into blossom.

CREATING SHADE

If you wish to turn a sun-baked area of your yard into a cool, shady one, or if the removal of a tree suddenly throws scorching sunlight down upon your shade garden, you can create instant shade by building garden structures.

Structures to create shade can be easy, straightforward, and inexpensive or expensive and elaborate. Among the least expensive solutions is to erect a structure of posts and beams and make a roof from greenhouse shade cloth, which is available in various densities. A more expensive but more attractive solution is to construct a wooden lath to rest on the rafters. These structures can be used to shade a planting bed, wooden deck, or a flagstone patio.

Intricate lath pergolas and arbors are elegant possibilities for creating shade for people and plants. They are designed to be covered with vines and are right at home in a lightly shaded setting, where they provide a perfect cool retreat.

If you build temporary shade structures, it's a good idea to also plant trees to provide future permanent shade. Select these trees carefully and you will be glad in the years to come. Choose trees that will branch high and provide an airy canopy of foliage, or plant more heavily foliaged trees and prune them as they mature. The trees described on page 11 have especially good manners in the shade garden.

CARING FOR BULBS

For the long-term benefit of bulbs in your garden, keep an eye out for deepening shade as high-branching trees form heavier canopies. Occasional thinning of branches may be necessary to keep the garden bright enough for the bulbs' foliage to mature properly, especially beneath early-leafing trees.

Spring bulbs, like most bulbs, require well-drained soil. If grading doesn't allow fast run-off, improve soil aeration by blending generous quantities of organic amendments like ground bark, peat moss, well-decayed compost, or nitrogen-supplemented sawdust into the soil to a depth of 4 or 5 inches. Even on slopes with runoff, it is a good idea to amend heavy soil.

Late summer to early autumn is the planting season for spring bulbs. If you must plant later (but never after cold weather has set in), plant deeper than usual and mulch heavily to permit root development in warm soil before winter. If you receive a shipment of bulbs too early for planting, store them in a cool, well-ventilated place until planting time. Refrigerating bulbs in paper (not plastic) bags is a suitable storage method.

Planting depths vary among spring bulbs. A generally sound rule of thumb is to cover them with soil whose depth is 1-1/2 to 2 times the diameter of the bulbs.

Like other plants in gardens shaded by trees, bulbs can suffer when competing with greedy, shallow-rooted trees for moisture and nutrients. The best solution, of course, is to avoid planting near such trees. But if you have no choice, then plant bulbs about 3 inches deeper than usual.

Avoid planting in areas where you will later dig to plant perennials or ground covers, or use stakes or rocks as markers.

Watering is important. When bulbs are planted, soil should be thoroughly watered unless it is already moist. From the time they sprout above ground level through the flowering period, soil should be moist. For deep bulbs this means thorough watering if soil is dry. Remember that bulbs growing among tree roots are most likely to be dry. When foliage becomes yellow and dry, stop watering for the rest of the season.

PESTS AND PROBLEMS

Certain insect pests and diseases are more troublesome in shady areas. Moist conditions favor fungal diseases such as powdery mildew and botrytis. Most fungal spores need a film of water to germinate in and sometimes even very high humidity will do. If breezes waft through your shade garden, the water on leaf surfaces evaporates and fungal spores don't get much of a chance. But if air circulates poorly and becomes stagnant, diseases will have an easy entrance.

Fungus diseases are best deterred by pruning to increase air circulation (see Air Circulation on page 26) and watering early in the day so flowers and foliage can dry before evening. It is also important to clean up infected plant debris from the ground, since this contains spores that will reinfect the plants.

If fungus diseases do attack, spraying with an appropriate fungicide can sometimes stop the infection. Most fungicides work best, however, at preventing an infection and can't eradicate it completely after it has begun. Where disease has been a recurrent problem, it is advisable to apply a fungicide periodically during the growing season, before any signs of the disease are present.

Plants growing in too much shade often produce softer, larger leaves that are more vulnerable to insect attack. Choosing plants that are well adapted to your climate and to the amount of shade where they are growing will help prevent insect problems. If insect problems occur and appear to be serious, consult your nurseryman for appropriate chemical controls.

Top-Rated Plants for Shady Gardens

Flowering dogwood (*Cornus* sp.) and English ivy (*Hedera helix*) thrive in the shade cast by towering canopy trees.

The list of plants that flourish in shady gardens is a long one. It includes almost every type of plant from the lowest-growing ground cover to small flowering trees. These plants offer the shade gardener every color in nature from the soft green of ferns to the bright colored blossoms of annuals, perennials, and bulbs.

The shade-loving plants described in the following charts were selected because of their top-rated growth performance and reliability in many areas of the United States. They are widely available in the climate zones where they are adapted.

The charts group the plants according to their most common landscape use, such as lawns and ground covers, or according to set botanical groups, such as ferns, annuals, or perennials. Since some plants fall into more than one category—for instance some ferns can also be used as ground covers and most wildflowers are also perennials—before you decide on which plant to buy, it may be helpful to glance through this entire chapter for additional ideas.

Each chart contains all the pertinent information necessary to select the right plants for your shady garden. The plants are listed in alphabetical order according to botanical name. The USDA zone recommendations and regional adaptation codes (see page 21) are given for each plant, along with cultural information.

Wisteria (*Wisteria* sp.)

American holly (*Ilex opaca*)

Star jasmine (*Trachelospermum* sp.)

Variegated euonymus (*Euonymus* sp.)

In mass plantings, the vividly colored foliage of coleus (*Coleus x hybridus*) makes shaded sites glow with living color.

Impatiens (*Impatiens wallerana*) are blanketed with blossoms all summer long, adding visual impact to shaded flower beds.

Annuals —plant each year.

Botanical/ Common Name	Zones and Regions	Type of Shade	Height	Plant Description	Comments/Uses
Antirrhinum majus Snapdragon	2-10 All regions.	Light.	6 in. to 3 ft.	Available in dwarf, semi-dwarf, medium, and tall varieties. Dark green, lance-shaped leaves to 3 in. long. Flowers on tall spikes, sac-like with petals forming upper and lower lips, appearing like dragon's jaws. Blooms from summer to frost, many colors, cinnamon-scented.	Space 6 to 8 in. apart, pinch shoots when young to encourage branching. Squeeze sides of flowers to make "jaws" open. Use for tall borders, background, rock gardens, or cut flowers. Used as a cool-season annual in mild-winter climates.
Begonia (fibrous-rooted) *B. x semperflorens-cultorum* Wax Begonia	2-10 All regions.	Light to half.	6-12 in.	Mounding habit. Leaves to 4 in. long, oval to heart-shaped, glossy, green to bronze, or green variegated with white. Flowers in clusters, single or double, white, pink or red. Blooms almost continuously.	Space 8 to 10 in. apart. Use for bedding, borders, or containers. See page 33 for varieties.
Clarkia amoena Farewell-to-Spring, Godetia	2-10 All regions.	Light to half.	18-24 in.	Sprawling habit. Leaves to 2 in. long, narrow, tapering. Flowers in axils of stems, to 3 in. across, single or double, cup-shaped, white, pink, salmon, purple through red. Blooms summer until frost.	Space 8 to 10 in. apart. Use as bedding plant, in containers. for cut flowers.
Coleus x hybridus Coleus	2-10 All regions.	Light to full.	6-36 in.	Dense habit. Leaves variable, 3-6 in. long, smooth or toothed edges, pointed, splashed with many combinations of colors. Flowers should be pinched off to encourage more leaf production.	Space 10 to 18 in. apart. Grown for unique foliage, not flowers. Use for borders, window boxes, planters, as houseplants. See chart on page 32 for varieties.
Impatiens wallerana Impatiens	2-10 All regions.	Light to full.	6-12 in.	Compact, mounding habit. Leaves are 1 to 3 in. long, oval, dark with lighter undersides. Dazzling flowers held above foliage in almost every shade, some bicolors. Blooms spring to fall.	One of the big 3 annuals for shade gardens. See page 34 for variety descriptions. New Guinea hybrids have brightly colored foliage.
Lobelia erinus Edging Lobelia	2-10 All regions.	Light to half.	6 in.	Trailing habit. Leaves to 1 in. long with serrated edges. Flowers to 3/4 in. across, white, blue, or pink, in summer.	Space 4 to 6 in. apart. Use for ground cover, edging, hanging basket, or borders.

Botanical/Common Name	Zones and Regions	Type of Shade	Height	Plant Description	Comments/Uses
Lobularia maritima Sweet Alyssum	2-10 All regions.	Light.	1 ft.	Mounding habit. Narrow leaves to 2 in. long. Flowers in small clusters, 4-petaled, fragrant, white, pink, rose, or purple. Blooms from summer until frost.	Space 6 to 8 in. apart. Use for borders, edging, planter boxes, rock gardens.
Mimulus species Monkey Flower	2-10 All regions.	Light to full.	1 ft.	Mounding habit. Leaves oval with pointed tips, serrated edges. Tubular, 2-in. flowers on spikes rising well above foliage. Yellow, maroon, or bronze streaked, spotted or splashed with yellow, brown or red, resembling monkey's faces. Blooms in summer.	Space 6 in. apart. Use in planter boxes, rock gardens, hanging baskets, borders. Pinch blooms after first flowering to induce flowering a second time.
Mysotis sylvatica (*M. alpestris*) Forget-Me-Not	2-10 All regions.	Light.	2 ft.	Clumplike habit. Leaves 2 in. long, narrow, hairy on upright stems. Blue, white, or pink flowers, 1/2 in. across, on stems held above foliage. Blooms in spring.	Space 8 to 12 in. apart. Use as background for spring flowers, in planter boxes, as ground cover. Sow seed in fall. Will self-sow.
Nemophila menziesii Baby-Blue-Eyes	2-10 All regions.	Light to full.	6-10 in.	Mounding habit. Leaves fern-like, finely divided, 2 in. long. Flowers 1-1/2 in. across, fragrant, trumpet-shaped, blue with white centers, at ends of short stems. Blooms in summer.	Space 6 to 9 in. apart. Use in rock gardens, as ground cover, border, edging.
Nicotiana alata Flowering Tobacco, Jasmine Tobacco	2-10 All regions.	Light to half.	2-3 ft.	Bushy habit. Leaves 4-10 in. long. Flowers are long, star-shaped, trumpetlike tubes that stand at right angles from the stem. Colors range from white through green to pink and lavender. Fragrant flowers appear from summer until frost.	Space 1 ft apart. Some varieties open only at night or on overcast days, others open midday. Plant where fragrance can be appreciated. Use massed in large beds, for borders, large containers.
Nierembergia species Cupflower	2-10 All regions.	Light.	6 in. to 3 ft.	*N. hippomanica*: compact, mounding habit, 6-12 in. high. Leaves narrow, stiff to 1/3 in. long. Flowers profuse, cup-shaped, 1 in. wide, violet-blue. Blooms in summer. *N. scoparia*: bushy, 2-3 ft high. Leaves to 3/4 in. long, narrow, stiff. Flowers profuse, cup-shaped, 1 in. across, blue with white tinge. Blooms in summer.	*N. hippomanica*: use as ground cover, rock gardens, edging or container plant. *N. scoparia*: use for planter boxes, rock gardens, backgrounds.
Nigella damascena Love-in-a-Mist	2-10 All regions.	Light.	1-2-1/2 ft.	Branching habit. Leaves thread-like, forming a collar under flowers. Blossoms single, at ends of stems, to 1-1/2 in. across, white, red, or blue. Blooms spring through summer. Fruit follows: globular seedpod, green with reddish markings.	Space 8 in. apart. Airy looking. Seeds used in flavoring foods. Flowers used for bedding and in cut arrangements.
Pelargonium species Geranium	2-10 All regions.	Light.	10 to 36 in.	Habit varies by type from bushy to trailing. Lobed green leaves often marked with contrasting zones or rings of dark or lighter green, bronze, pink, or white. Bright colored round flowers clusters in many shades of white, pink, and red held above the foliage on strong stems. Perennial in Zones 9-10.	Space 12 to 24 inches apart. Many species available some with scented leaves. Lady Washington, Geranium, *P. x domesticum* is very popular in warm climates. Ivy geranium, *P. peltatum,* has a sprawling habit; excellent as a ground cover or hanging basket. All geraniums are beautiful border or pot plants and flower best in full sun but also do well in partial shade.
Petunia x hybrida Petunia	2-10 All regions.	Half to light.	12-14 in.	Downy leaved, mounding or cascading plants bear brightly colored, single or double trumpet-shaped blossoms in almost every color; many bicolors. Blooms from late spring to frost.	Divided into 2 types; multi-floras (more but smaller flowers) and grandifloras (larger but fewer flowers.) Many varieties available. Some have cascading habits ideal for containers. Space 8 to 12 inches apart. Pinch back and fertilize if plants get too leggy.

Annuals (continued)

Botanical/ Common Name	Zones and Regions	Type of Shade	Height	Plant Description	Comments/Uses
Primula malacoides Fairy Primrose	2-10 All regions.	Light to full.	12-15 in.	Low-growing rosette of rounded hairy leaves. Flowers on slender stems in whorls, delicate appearance. Blooms in soft shades of lavender, pink, white, and red in early spring.	Grows best in cool, moist conditions. Excellent woodland plant or combined with early spring bulbs.
P. x polyantha Polyanthus Primrose	2-10 All regions.	Light to full.	6-12 in.	Basal rosette of 4- to 6-in. tongue-shaped leaves with rich green crinkled texture. Fragrant flowers 1 to 2 inches across in large clusters, on thick, erect stems. Pure red, purple, yellow, pink, bronze, apricot, and maroon. All with yellow eye, some gold-edged, or double. Blooms in spring.	A most popular bedding or pot plant. Space 6 to 12 inches apart. Plants short-lived but divide easily every 1 to 2 years. Plants die back, resprout in early spring. Best in cool, moist areas.
Salvia splendens Scarlet Sage	2-10 All regions.	Light to half.	1-3 ft.	Bushy, branching habit. Leaves 3 in. long, oval, pointed, glossy, deep green. Flowers on spikes, held above foliage, 1 in. long, tubular, white, rose through scarlet to lavender, from early summer until frost.	Space 8 to 12 in. apart. Use massed in shade garden, borders, edging, planter boxes.
Torenia fournieri Wishbone Flower, Bluewings	2-10 All regions.	Light to full.	12 in.	Loose, clumplike habit. Leaves 2 in. long with toothed edges. Flowers 1 in. across, on winged stalks, are divided into light purple upper lip, dark purple lower lip. Yellow throat has wishbone-shaped stamens. Blooms from summer until frost.	Space 6 to 8 in. apart. Use for borders, edging, planter boxes, houseplant.

Coleus

CAREFREE Small leaves, deeply lobed.

DRAGON Large leaves, moderately lobed.

FIJI Large leaves, delicately fringed.

PONCHO SERIES Cascading, for hanging baskets.

RAINBOW Large leaves, heart-shaped.

RAINBOW, FRINGE-LEAVED Similar to Rainbow, leaves fringed.

SABER Long, saber-shaped leaves.

WIZARD Large leaves, heart-shaped.

Wax begonia (*Begonia x semperflorens-cultorum*)

Hybrid tuberous begonia (*Begonia x tuberhybrida*)

Hybrid tuberous begonia (*Begonia x tuberhybrida*)

Begonia

Series or Variety	Height	Foliage	Flowers
WAX BEGONIA			
Cocktail series:			
'Brandy'	6-8 in.	Bronze.	Light pink.
'Gin'	6-8 in.	Bronze-green.	Rose.
'Vodka'	6-8 in.	Bronze.	Deep scarlet.
'Whisky'	6-8 in.	Bronze.	White.
'Gladiator'	12-18 in.	Bronze-tinted green.	Red.
Glamour Series	8-10 in.	Green.	Pink, red, rose, white, and white edged with rose. Large.
'Indian Maid'	6-8 in.	Bronze.	Scarlet.
'Linda'	6-8 in.	Green.	Deep rose.
'Othello'	6-8 in.	Dark bronze.	Scarlet-orange.
'Scarletta'	6-8 in.	Green.	Large, scarlet.
'Snowbank'	8-10 in.	Green.	White.
Thousand Wonders (Tausendschon) Series	6-8 in.	Green.	Scarlet, white.
'Viva'	6-8 in.	Green.	White.

Series, Variety, or Type	Form	Colors	Comments
HYBRID TUBEROUS			
Camellia	Upright.	White, pink, red, yellow, orange, scarlet, salmon, deep red, apricot.	Large, ruffled double flowers resemble camellias.
Carnation	Upright.	Deep red, pink, white, orange, yellow.	Large, ruffled, frilly flowers resemble carnations.
Crispa Marginata	Upright.	Bicolors: yellow edged with crimson, white edged with crimson.	Large, frilled single flowers.
Multiflora Maxima	Upright.	Orange, yellow, red, white, pink.	Multitudes of 2-in. single or double flowers on sun-tolerant plants; excellent for beds or pots.
Nonstop	Upright.	Yellow, red, orange, pink, rose, apricot, salmon.	Double, semidouble, and a few single flowers on same plants. Compact growth habit. Very free-flowering.
Picotee Double	Upright.	Bicolors: white edged with pink, red, or apricot. 'Flamenco' speckled red and white. 'Sunburst' yellow edged with red.	Flowers are large and ruffled.
Rose Form	Upright.	Apricot, pink, yellow, white, red, salmon.	Edges of petals smooth, center petals furled like center of rose.
Ruffled Double (Ballerina)	Upright.	Apricot, yellow, white, pink, scarlet.	Flowers heavily ruffled, 6 to 8 inches wide.
Hanging Basket	Pendulous.	Pink, red, yellow, orange, apricot; picotee types: assorted pastel colors with red or pink edge.	Many Belgian hybrids have slender leaves and wide-open flowers with attractively slender petals. American hybrids have rounder petals. Various Hanging Basket begonias sometimes marketed as Lloydii or Lloydii Pendula begonias.
Happy End	Pendulous.	Red, orange, salmon, white.	This series of pendulous begonias has a mixture of single and double flowers.
Sensations	Pendulous.	Red, yellow, copper, white, pink.	This series of pendulous begonias has large double flowers.

Impatiens *(Impatiens wallerana)* is a choice plant for creating a sparkling display of vibrant color in shady garden areas. Blossoms blanket plants all during the summer season.

Impatiens

Series or Variety	Colors	Comments
DWARF (8-10 in.)		
Super Elfin	Fuchsia, orange, orchid, rose, pink, hot pink, scarlet, salmon, red, white, bicolors.	Profuse flowering, good branching at base of plants, and very compact habit make this series especially suitable for hanging baskets and pots as well as beds. 'Blush' is delicate pink with red eye; 'Lipstick', deep rose with white eye. Others are named for colors. Super Elfin varieties are also sold as a mix.
INTERMEDIATE (10-12 in.)		
Futura	Burgundy, coral, orange, orchid, pink, red, rose-pink, scarlet, white, pale rose.	The all-time favorite series, useful for hanging baskets, planters, and beds. Growth habit is compact and mounding. Varieties are named for colors; often sold as a mix. 'Wild Rose' is especially iridescent.
Novette	Bright orange, deep orange ('Scarlet'), orange, deep rose, pink, red, salmon, violet, white, bicolor.	Same growth habit and uses as Futura series. 'Rose & White Star' is bicolored. 'Bright Orange' has bronze leaves.
Twinkles	White-star pattern on fuchsia, red, rose, scarlet.	Same growth habit and uses as Futura and Novette series. Sold by color names or as a mix.
TALL (12-16 in.)		
'Blitz'	Intense scarlet.	Other impatiens have 1- to 2-in. flowers, but 'Blitz' has 2-1/2-in. ones. Bronze foliage. Excellent in beds and hanging baskets. An award winner.
Duet	White with red, scarlet, and deep rose.	Double and semidouble bicolored flowers on large, relatively upright plants. Useful for beds and large containers. Sold as a mix. Can grow taller than other tall impatiens—to 18-20 in.
Grandé	Coral, orange, orchid, purple, red, rose, white.	Large flowers on plants suitable for all uses. Sold by color names or as a mix.
'Tangeglow'	Very bright orange.	Suitable for all uses.
Zigzag	White with scarlet, orange, pink, rose, salmon, or purple.	Striking bicolors sold as a mix. Suitable for all uses.

Biennials and Perennials

Botanical/ Common Name	Zones and Regions	Type of Shade	Height	Plant Description	Comments/Uses
Aconitum carmichaelii Monkshood	See wildflowers page 40.				
Alyssum montanum Madwort *A. saxatile* — see *Aurinia*	4-10 All regions.	Light.	6-10 in.	Mounding habit. Leaves silvery-gray, covered with dense hairs. Bright yellow, fragrant flowers on stems held above foliage. Blooms spring into summer.	Space 6 in. apart. Use for edging or rock gardens.
Anchusa azurea Alkanet, Bugloss	4-10 All regions.	Light.	3-5 ft.	Open, spreading habit. Leaves to 6 in. long, oval to lance-shaped, covered with stiff hairs. Flowers in clusters, 3/4 in. across, bright blue. Blooms in summer.	Space 1 to 2 ft apart. Use for borders, as bedding plants.
Anemone x hybrida (*A. hupensis japonica*) Japanese Anemone	6-9 All regions.	Light to half.	2-1/2 ft.	Clumplike habit. Leaves to 5 in. long, deeply lobed (maple-like) with toothed edges, dark green. Flowers on tall stems held well above foliage, 3 in. across, white to pink. Blooms late summer until frost.	Space 6 to 15 in. apart. Use for borders, background, rock gardens, containers, and cut flowers.
Aquilegia x hybrida Columbine	3-9 A-I	Light.	2-3 ft.	Erect, branching habit. Leaves lobed, blue-green, lacy. Flowers to 3 in. across with spurs. Wide range of colors including bicolors. Blooms in early summer.	Space 1 to 2 ft apart. Use for borders, rock gardens, under trees, as cut flowers. Hummingbirds attracted to blooms.
Arabis caucasica Rock Cress	6-10 All regions.	Light.	6 in.	Mounding to matlike habit. Leaves soft, gray-green. Flowers to 1/2 in. across, fragrant, white, in spring.	Space 10 to 12 in. apart. Use for borders, edging, rock gardens, walls.
Aster species Asters, Michaelmas Daisy	4-10 All regions.	Light.	9 in. to 6 ft.	Mounding to bushy habit. Leaves variable—1/2 to 5 in. long. Flowers to 2 in. across, daisy-like. Blooming season variable, according to species.	Space 12 to 15 in. apart. Use for rock gardens, borders, containers, cut flowers. *A. alpinus*: 9 in. high, flowers white, lavender, or blue. Blooms in late summer. *A. novae-angliae*: 3-5 ft high, leaves to 5 in. long, flowers red to purple. Blooms in late summer. *A. novi-belgii*: 3-4 ft high, flowers white, pink, lavender, or blue. Blooms in fall.
Astilbe x arendsii False Spiraea	4-9 A,B,F, G,H,I	Light to full.	6-30 in.	Mounding habit to 1-1/2 ft high. Leaves fernlike, with toothed edges. Fluffy, white, pink to red flowers held on spikes above foliage. Blooms in summer.	Space 1 to 2 ft apart. Use for borders, as cut flowers, can be dried. Effective near pools.
Aurinia saxatilis Basket-of-Gold	3-10 All regions.	Light.	6-12 in.	Mounding habit. Leaves silvery-gray, covered with dense hairs. Flowers on stems held above foliage, bright yellow. Blooms in spring.	Space 6 in. apart. Use for edging or rock gardens.
Begonia (rhizomatous-rooted) *B. x rex-cultorum* Rex Begonia	2-10 All regions.	Light to half.	10-18 in.	Leaves emerge from stems at or slightly below ground level. Leaves 8-12 in. long, heart shaped with toothed edges, very showy with many colors in exotic designs. Flowers insignificant, white to pink.	Space 12 in. apart. Requires humidity. Use in containers and as houseplant.
Bergenia cordifolia Heartleaf Bergenia	2-10 A,B,C,F, G,H,I,J	Light to full.	12-18 in.	Clumplike habit. Leaves to 10 in. wide, thick, heart-shaped to round (similar to cabbage), dark green with crisped, wavy edges. Flowers to 3/4 in. across, in clusters on thick stems, at or just above foliage. Colors range from white through rose-pink to purple.	Space 12 to 15 in. apart. Use for rock gardens, borders, near ponds. Requires humidity.

Shade-loving annuals, perennials, and bulbs combine well together.

Foxglove (*Digitalis purpurea*)

Forget-me-not (Mysotis sp.)

Biennials and Perennials (continued)

Botanical/Common Name	Zones and Regions	Type of Shade	Height	Plant Description	Comments/Uses
Brunnera macrophylla Siberian Bugloss	3-10 All regions.	Light to half.	1-1/2 ft.	Clumplike habit. Leaves 6-8 in. long, heart-shaped, dark green. Flowers on thin stems held above foliage, 1/4 in. across, in small clusters, blue with yellow centers. Blooms in spring.	Space 12 to 18 in. apart. Use under trees, in between evergreen shrubs for touch of color.
***Campanula* species** Bellflower	3-8* A,B,C, F,G,H,I	Light to half.	From 6 to 48 in. high, rounded to spreading.	Leaves to 1 in. long, heart-shaped with serrated edges. Flowers bell-shaped to star-shaped, pale blue to white.	Many species available. *C. glomerata* reaches 1-1/2 to 2-1/2 ft and is spreading. Blooms spring to midsummer and is a good cut flower. *C. isophylla* reaches 2 ft high and blooms midsummer to fall. *C. medium*, a biennial, grows 6 to 12 in. high with tall flower stalks from spring to midsummer. For other species see the ground cover chart on page 54.
***Cyclamen* species** Hardy Cyclamen	5-10 A,B,C, F,G,H,I	Light to half.	To 10 in.	Small clumplike habit. Leaves to 3 in. wide, round to heart-shaped, variegated with silver, light and dark green. Flowers 1-2 in., nodding, petals reflexed. Succulent stems carry flowers above foliage. Colors range from white through pink to purple. Some varieties are fragrant. Blooms in spring and fall.	Space 3 to 6 in. apart. Use for borders, rock gardens, containers. Many species available.
Dicentra spectabilis Bleeding-Heart	4-8 A,B,C,F, G,H,I,J	Light to half.	2-3 ft.	Mounding habit. Soft green leaves on arching stems, finely cut with smooth edges.	Space 2 ft apart. Better as single plant than massed. Also a good chocie for wildflower garden.
Digitalis purpurea Common Foxglove	4-10 All regions.	Light to full.	To 5 ft.	Basal clump of large oval leaves with pointed leaf tips, dark green above, light green beneath. Tubular, 3-in.-long, white, yellow, pink, purple, or red flowers with spotted throats on tall spikes. Blooms spring and summer.	Space 15 to 24 in. apart. Use for background, borders, as cut flowers. All plant parts poisonous. Stake flower spikes individually. May act as biennial or perennial.
Doronicum cordatum Leopard's-Bane	4-10 A,B,F, G,H,I,J	Light.	2-3 ft.	Clumplike habit. Leaves 3-5 in. long, heart-shaped with toothed edges. Single, 2- to 3-in., daisylike, bright yellow flowers on long stems. Blooms in spring and summer.	Space 12 to 15 in. apart. Use for borders, rock gardens, as cut flowers.
Helleborus niger Christmas Rose	4-10 A,B,C, D,E,F, G,H,I	Light to half.	1-1/2 ft.	Clumplike habit. Leaves divided into 7-9 toothed, dark green leaflets. Flowers 2-4 in. across, roselike, white to pink with yellow-tipped stamens, fall through spring.	Best used as single plants, not massed. Sensitive to transplanting. Mix with other shade-loving plants for fall and winter bloom.

Botanical/Common Name	Zones and Regions	Type of Shade	Height	Plant Description	Comments/Uses
Hemerocallis hybrids Daylily	3-10 All regions.	Light to half.	2-5 ft.	Clumplike habit. Leaves 1-2 ft long, narrow, arching. Lily-like flowers, 3-5 in. across, on tall spikes, arising from mound of foliage. Colors range from yellow, orange, pink through red to maroon. Blooms in summer, each flower lasting only 1 day, but a profusion of flowers over a long season.	Space 18-36 in. apart. Use for borders, under deciduous trees, near pools, etc. Choose early, mid-, or late season varieties.
Heuchera sanguinea Coralbells	4-10 All regions.	Light to half.	2 ft.	Mounding habit. Leaves 1-2 in. wide, heart-shaped with scalloped edges. Flowers on tall wiry stems, 1/2 in. across, bellshaped, pink to red. Blooms in summer.	Space 9 to 15 in. apart. Use for edging, rock gardens, cut flowers.
Hosta ventricosa (*H. caerula*) Blue Plantain Lily	4-9 A,B,C, D,F,G, H,I,J	Light to full.	3 ft.	Clumplike habit. Leaves to 9 in. long, heart-shaped, shiny blue-green. Spikes of violet or blue, bell-shaped, 2-in., flowers on 3-ft-tall spikes. Blooms in late summer.	Space 1 ft apart. Use for ground cover, edging, borders, containers. Valued primarily for striking foliage. See ground covers (page 55) for other hosta species.
Iberis sempervirens Edging Candytuft	4-10 All regions.	Light.	12 in.	Compact, mounding habit. Leaves to 1-1/2 in. long, narrow, dark green. White flowers in clusters above foliage, spring into summer, sometimes repeating in fall.	Space 6 to 9 in. apart. Use for ground cover, edging, borders, rock gardens, or containers.
Iris kaempferi Japanese Iris	5-9 A,B,F, G,H,I,J	Light to half.	3-5 ft.	Upright habit. Leaves sword-shaped, 3 ft long. Flowers on stems growing above foliage, to 8 in. across with reflexed sepals on a horizontal plane. Colors range from white through pink to purple and blue. Blooms in summer.	Space 18 in. apart. Excellent for cut flowers, borders, rock gardens, along fences. Needs moisture and grows in boggy soil at edge of pond.
Lobelia cardinalis Cardinal Flower	4-10	Light to half.	3 ft.	Upright habit. Leaves 4 in. long, narrow, pointed with serrated edges, along upright stems. Flowers at tops of stems, tubular, intense red, in summer.	Space 15 to 18 in. apart. Requires moist soil. Use for borders, edging, along streams.
Mertensia virginica Virginia Bluebells	See wildflowers page 41.				
Myosotis scorpioides (*M. palustris*) Forget-Me-Not	4-10 All regions.	Light.	1-1/2 ft.	Upright habit. Narrow, 2-in.-long leaves along upright stems. Flowers 1/4 in. across, bright blue with white, yellow or pink centers. Blooms in summer.	Space 8 to 12 in. apart. Spreads by creeping stems. Use for background, edging, ground cover, planter boxes.
Paeonia hybrids Chinese Peony, Common Garden Peony	5-8 A,B,F, G,H,I,J	Light.	2-4 ft.	Clumplike habit. Leaves large, divided or lobed, with narrow leaflets. Flowers held on stems above leaves, 1-8 in. across, single to double, white through pink to red. Blooms in summer.	Old-fashioned favorite. Use for borders, background, excellent cut flower. Best in cool-summer climates.
Polygonatum odoratum Solomon's-Seal	See wildflowers page 41.				
Saxifraga stolonifera Strawberry Geranium, Mother-of-Thousands	8-10 B,C,J,I	Light to half.	1-1/2- 2 ft.	Low mound to matlike habit. Hairy leaves to 4 in. across, in rosettes, white-veined with reddish undersides. Young plantlets form on ends of slender runners as with strawberries. White, 1-in. flowers in clusters on tall branching stems. Blooms in spring.	Space 6 to 12 in. apart. Use for ground cover, in hanging baskets, rock gardens, as houseplant.
Trollius europaeus Globeflower	5-10 All regions.	Light to full.	1-2 ft.	Bushy habit. Dark green leaves divided into 3-5 lobes. Flowers 1-3 in. across, globe shaped, yellow to orange on ends of long stems. Blooms spring through summer.	Space 1 ft apart. Use near pools and ponds, to brighten shade areas, as cut flowers. Needs ample moisture.
Viola odorata Sweet Violet	See wildflowers page 41, and ground covers page 57.				

Tender Bulbs

Botanical/Common Name	Zones and Regions	Type of Shade	Height	Plant Description	Comments
Agapanthus species Lily-of-the-Nile	Perennial in 9-10. Annual elsewhere.	Light to half.	15-48 in.	Dark green, straplike leaves. Clusters of bright blue, trumpet-shaped flowers borne on tall stalks in summer.	*A. orientalis* grows to 48 inches high. *A.* x 'Peter Pan' reaches only 15 inches.
Begonia (tuberous-rooted) *B.* x *tuberhybrida*	Perennial in 9-10. Annual elsewhere.	Light to half.	12-18 in. Pendulous.	Leaves emerge from tubers, to 6 in. long, round to heart-shaped, pointed with crisped edges, dark green. Flowers to 8 in. across single or double; white, vivid yellow, pink, apricot, orange, or red.	Space 8 to 10 in. apart. Requires humidity. Use in hanging baskets, for borders, as houseplant. Stake upright types. See page 33 for varieties.
Caladium x *hortulanum* Fancy-Leaved Caladium	Perennial in 10. Annual elsewhere.	Light to full.	12-24 in.	Grown for its dramatic heart-shaped leaves mottled or blotched in shades of white, green, red, pink, or bronze.	Must have well-drained soil.
Zantedeschia aethiopica Calla Lily	Perennial in 8-10. Annual elsewhere.	Light to half.	36-48 in.	Beautiful dark green, arrow-shaped leaves. Large white, funnel-shaped flowers in spring and summer.	Best in moist soil. Some dwarf forms often available.

Spring-Blooming Bulbs

Botanical/Common Name	Zones and Regions	Type of Shade	Height	Plant Description	Comments
Chionodoxa luciliae Glory-of-the-Snow	3-8 A,B,F, G,H,I	Light to half.	6 in.	Each plant produces 2 or more ribbonlike leaves. Bright blue, star-shaped flowers with white centers borne in early spring.	Naturalizes freely from seed. *C. sardensis* has darker blue flowers.
Clivia miniata Kaffir Lily	9-10 B,C,D,J	Light to full.	12-18 in.	Mounding, dense habit. Leaves lilylike, to 18 in. long, 3 in. wide, fleshy, dark green. Flowers in big clusters on stems just above foliage, 2-3 in. across, intense orange with yellow-tipped stamens, in spring.	Use for planter boxes, containers, as best bloom occurs when tuberous roots are crowded.
Convallaria majalis Lily-of-the-Valley	See ground covers page 54.				
Crocus Crocus species	3-10 in. All regions.	Light.	5 in.	Small grasslike leaves. Cupped flowers in a multitude of colors. Blooms in early spring or fall.	Many species available. Best in cold climates.
Endymion hispanicus Blue Bells	4-10 All regions.	Light.	18 in.	Bright green straplike leaves. Tall spikes of bright blue, bell-shaped flowers in spring.	Often sold as a species of *Scilla*.
Eranthis hyemalis Winter Aconite	4-8 A,B,F, G,H,I	Light to half.	4 in.	Delicate, finely cut foliage. Small buttery yellow, cup-shaped flowers in mid- to late winter.	Blooms through snow. Naturalizes quickly.
Galanthus species Snowdrops	3-9 A,B,F, G,H,I	Light.	9-12 in.	Grasslike foliage. Nodding white flowers are dotted green on inner petals. Bloom in early spring.	Two species most common are *G. nivalis* with 3/4 to 1 inch long flowers and leaves 1/4 inch wide; and *G. elwessi* with clumps of 1-1/2-inch-long flowers and 3/4-inch-wide leaves.
Leujocum vernum Spring Snowflake	5-8 A,B,F, G,H,I	Light.	9-12 in.	Bright green grass-like leaves. White, bell-shaped flowers, spotted green bloom in early spring.	Very similar to snowdrop. Naturalizes freely.
Muscari species Grape Hyacinth	3-10 All regions.	Light.	6-12 in.	Thin, grasslike leaves. Short spikes of sweetly scented, blue to purple flowers in spring.	Several species of similar plants. Naturalizes freely.
Narcissus species Daffodil, Jonquil, Narcissus	5-10 All regions.	Light.	5-20 in.	Bright green, grasslike foliage. A multitude of flower shapes and sizes. May be fragrant. Blooms in spring, primarily in shades of white, yellow an orange.	A large family of very popular bulbs. Some naturalize.

Caladium (*Caladium x hortulanum*)

Grape hyacinths (*Muscari* sp.)

Easter lily (*Lilium longiflorum*)

Botanical/ Common Name	Zones and Regions	Type of Shade	Height	Plant Description	Comments
Scilla siberica Siberian Scilla, Siberian Squill	3-8 A,B,F, G,H,I	Light.	6 in.	Bright green, grasslike foliage. Delicate, bell-shaped blue flowers on short spikes in early spring.	Naturalizes quickly in moist soil.
***Tulipa* species** Tulip	5-9 All regions.	Light.	8-30 in. inches.	Short, straplike leaves. Single blooms on tall stems borne in a rainbow of colors and many shapes. Blooms from spring into summer depending on type.	Many species and hybrids available. Requires cold storage before planting to bloom in mild climate.

Bulbs That Bloom in Late Spring, Summer, or Fall

Botanical/ Common Name	Zones and Regions	Type of Shade	Height	Plant Description	Comments
***Cyclamen* species** Hardy Cyclamen	5-10 A,B,C, F,G,H,I	Light to half.	To 10 in.	Small clumplike habit. Leaves to 3 in. wide, round to heart-shaped, variegated with silver, light and dark green. Flowers 1-2 in., nodding, petals reflexed. Succulent stems carry flowers above foliage. Colors range from white through pink to purple. Some varieties are fragrant. Blooms in spring and fall.	Space 3 to 6 in. apart. Use for borders, rock gardens, containers. Many species available.
Fritillaria imperialis Crown Imperial Fritillaria	5-8 A,B,F, G,H,I	Light.	2-4 ft.	Unusual foliage arranged in a pineapplelike tuft. Clusters of orange, red, or yellow nodding flowers on tall stalks in late spring.	*F. meleagris*, bears a purple checked flower in spring.
***Lilium* species** Lilies	4-10 All regions.	Light to half.	1-7 ft.	Erect stalks lined with thin green leaves. Trumpet-shaped flowers in a variety of colors; some fragrant. Blooms in summer.	The classic summer-blooming bulb. Many species and hybrids available. Grows best in moist soil.
Lycoris squamigera Magic Lily	6-10 All regions.	Light.	15-24 in.	Thin, strapped-shaped leaves. Spidery clusters of fragrant rose-pink flowers borne atop tall stalks in fall.	Best in well-drained soil that dries out in summer.
Nerine bowdenii Nerine	8-10 A,B,C, I,J	Light.	15-20 in.	Straplike foliage appears with or after flowers. Clusters of star-shaped, pink to magenta flowers on tall stalks in late summer.	Best in dry, sandy soil. Good in containers.
Ornithogalum umbellatum Star of Bethlehem	5-10 A,B,C, D,E,G, H,I,J	Light.	12 in.	Grasslike foliage. Clusters of white, star-shaped flowers borne on tall stalks in late spring.	Spreads rapidly. May be weedy in neat gardens.

Columbine (*Aquilegia* species), a charming and widely adapted wildflower, blooms in late spring and early summer.

The beguiling fringed flowers of bleeding heart (*Dicentra eximia*) lend sparkling color to shady spots all during their extended blooming season.

Wildflowers

Botanical/Common Name	Zones and Regions	Type of Plant	Type of Shade	Height	Plant Description	Comments
Aconitum carmichaelii Monkshood	4-9 A,B,F, G,H,I	Perennial.	Light to half.	3-4 ft.	Leaves dense, 2-6 in. long, leathery, deeply lobed, coarsely toothed near leaf tips, dark green. Spikes of helmet-shaped, bluish-purple flowers. Blooms late summer to fall.	All plant parts poisonous if eaten. Space 12 to 16 in. apart. Difficult to transplant. Use under trees, bordering shade garden, near water.
Aquilegia species Columbine	3-9 A,B,C, D,E,F, G,H,I	Perennial.	Light.	8 to 48 in.	Delicately lobed soft green leaves on a clumping plant. Stunning shooting-starlike flowers with back-sweeping, spurred petals bloom in late spring and early summer. Available in a rainbow of single and bicolored shades.	Many species available native to different parts of America. Choose local kinds. Sow seed in fall or use transplants in spring.
Cornus canadensis Bunchberry	2-7 A,B, F,G,H	Perennial.	Light to full.	6 to 10 in.	Whorls of bright green leaves on erect branches originate from vigorously spreading underground stems. White flowers with 4 to 6 petals appear in late spring followed by bright red berries.	Useful woodland ground cover in moist acid soils. Spreads rapidly.
Dicentra species Bleeding Heart	4-8 A,B,F, G,H,I	Perennials.	Light to half.	12 to 60 in.	Mounding habit. Soft green to grayish-green finely cut leaves. Pink to rose, yellow or white flowers on arching stems in spring and summer.	Several native species from different parts of the country. Try the rose-flowered fringed bleeding heart (*D. eximia*) in the East; Golden teardrops (*D. chrysantha*) or Western bleeding heart (*D. formosa*) in the West.
Erythronium dens-canis Dog-Tooth Violet	3-9 G,H,I		Light to half.	6 in.	Straplike leaves with reddish-brown mottling. Gracefully nodding, rose or purple, lily-like flower in spring.	Best in cool, moist soil. Other species sometimes available.

Wild sweet William (*Phlox divaricata*) spreads by underground shoots to form tidy mounds. Its copious blossoms are colorful and softly scented.

Sweet violets (*Viola odorata*) form a lush carpet of colorful blooms in spring, and seem most at home in the light shade of a natural woodland setting.

Botanical/ Common Name	Zones and Regions	Type of Plant	Type of Shade	Height	Plant Description	Comments
Mertensia virginica Virginia Bluebells	4-8 A,B,F, G,H,I	Perennial.	Light to full.	1 to 2 ft.	Upright habit. Leaves along stems to 7 in. long, lance-shaped with rounded ends. Nodding, 1-in.-long, trumpet-shaped flowers in clusters at ends of stems open pink maturing to light blue. Blooms in spring.	Space 8 to 12 in. apart. Plants die back by midsummer. Use interplanted with ferns. Requires moist soil.
Phlox divaricata Blue Phlox, Wild Sweet William	3-9 A,B,F, G,H,I,J	Perennial. May be evergreen.	Light.	12 to 18 in.	Oval leaves arising from spreading underground shoots. Loose clusters of violet-blue, pink, lavender or white flowers blanket plants in midspring. Lightly scented.	Beautiful ground cover. Plant from root cuttings in moist acid soil.
Polygonatum odoratum Solomon's-Seal	4-8 A,B,F, G,H,I	Perennial.	Light to full.	1-1/2 ft.	Erect, arching stems display 4-in.-long leaves alternately. One-in.-long, tubular flowers in pairs hang beneath leaf axils along stem; fragrant, greenish-white, in spring.	Space 12 to 18 in. apart. Spreads from creeping underground stems. *P.o.* 'Variegatum': leaves with white edges. Use with hosta, ferns for low-growing shade garden focal points. Best in cool-summer climates.
Sanguinaria canadensis Bloodroot	4-7, A,F, G,H,I	Perennial.	Light to full.	6 to 8 in.	Deeply lobed grayish-green leaves arising from spreading underground stems which exude a red juice when cut. White to pinkish flowers borne atop short stalks in spring.	Grows best in moist, acid soils. Propagate from seed or division.
Trillium species Wake Robin	4-8 A,B,F, G,H,I	Perennial.	Full.	6 to 18 in.	Fleshy underground stems produce a whorl of 3 oval leaves. White to greenish white, yellow or pinkish flowers in spring followed by often colorful berries. Some flowers fragrant.	Many species native to several areas of North America. Look for locally adapted types. Most grow best in moist acid soil. Grow from seeds or root cuttings.
Viola odorata Sweet Violet	6-10 All regions.	Perennial.	Light to half.	8 in.	Broadly clumping habit. Leaves 2-8 in. long, heart-shaped with toothed margins. Flowers 1 in. across, bright to deep blue, fragrant. Blooms in spring.	Spreads by rooting runners. Use for borders, edging, rock gardens, woodlands, beneath high-shade shrubs.

Also see *Primula* in the annual chart, page 32, and *Campanula* in the perennial chart, page 36 and the ground cover chart on page 54.

Ferns

Botanical/Common Name	Zones and Regions	Evergreen/Deciduous	Type of Shade	Size and Form	Plant Description	Comments/Uses
Adiantum pedatum Maidenhair Fern	3-8 A,B,F,G,H,I	Deciduous.	Light to half.	10 to 20 in., creeping.	Fronds finely divided. Black, wiry stems fork at ends, making graceful arching U-shape. Leaflets fan-shaped, notched, bluish-green.	One of many maidenhair ferns. Beautiful, lacy effect. Use in rock gardens, borders, wildflower garden.
Asplenium bulbiferum Mother Fern	9-10 B,C,J	Evergreen.	Light to full.	1 to 3 ft, rounded.	Fronds to 3 ft, arching, finely divided, light green.	Usually grown as houseplant. Plantlets grow on upper surface of fronds, can be removed and planted. Exotic looking.
A. nidus Bird's-Nest Fern	10 C,J	Evergreen.	Light to full.	1 to 4 ft.	Fronds to 4 ft long, undivided, stiff, upright, soft green, often with wavy edges.	Usually grown as houseplant. Fronds combine in a pattern to look somewhat like bird's nest. Fronds turn brown if handled.
A. trichomanes Maidenhair Spleenwort	3-8 A,B,C,D,E,F,G,H,I	Evergreen.	Light to full.	1 ft, upright.	Fronds once-divided, to 8 in. long, 3/4 in. wide. Leaflets round, 1/3 in., sometimes toothed. Stems black.	Withstands dryness for short periods. Unusually hardy. Often used in crevices of rock walls.
Athyrium filix-femina Lady Fern	3-8 A,B,C,D,E,F,G,H	Deciduous.	Light to half.	To 3 ft, creeping.	Fronds finely divided, upright, light green. Leaflets toothed.	Many cultivars available. Hardy. Can take full sun. Spreads by underground stems. Use for filling gaps between woodland plants.
Cibotium glaucum Hawaiian Tree Fern, Hapu	10 B,C,J	Evergreen.	Light to half.	15-ft tree fern.	Trunk covered with lustrous, yellowish-brown, matted hairs. Fronds long, finely divided, arching, smooth with no hairs, gray-green beneath.	Can be propagated by sections of trunk placed upright in moist medium until roots sprout. Majestic-looking accent plant for landscapes.
Cystopteris bulbifera Berry Bladder Fern	4-9 A,B,F,G,H,I	Deciduous.	Light to full.	1 to 3 ft.	Long fronds taper daintily, their undersides covered with bulblets which form new plants if planted during summer. Foliage is deep green.	Will grow in boggy and limestone soils. In natural habitat, grows in boggy soil along streams and in moist limestone cliffs.
Cyrtomium falcatum Holly Fern	8-10 B,C,I,J	Evergreen.	Light to full.	To 3 ft, upright, rounded.	Fronds to 3 ft long, with coarse hairs along stem. Once-divided. Leaflets to 5 in. long, holly-like, dark green and glossy.	Tolerates sun if kept moist. Use where bold, not lacy, effect is desired.
Davallia trichomanoides Squirrel's-Foot Fern	10 B,C,J	Evergreen to semi-deciduous.	Light to half.	1 ft, creeping.	Rhizomes covered with white to tan-brown hairs, hence the name. Fronds finely divided to 12 in. long, half as wide.	Epiphyte, usually grown in hanging baskets or as ground cover in Southern California.
Dicksonia antarctica Tasmanian Tree Fern, New Zealand Tree Fern	8-10 B,C,I,J	Evergreen.	Light to half.	To 30 ft, tree fern.	Trunk brown, covered with hairs. Fronds to 6 ft, finely divided, deep green.	Hardiest of tree ferns. In coastal areas can take full sun if kept moist. Protect from wind. Can be grown in tubs.
Dryopteris austriaca spinulosa Spinulose Wood Fern, Toothed Wood Fern	5-10 All regions.	Evergreen to semi-deciduous.	Light to full.	To 3 ft.	Fronds to 2 ft long, finely divided. Leaflets spiny-toothed.	Used by florists for cut-flower arrangements.
D. erythrosora Japanese Shield Fern, Wood Fern	5-10 All regions.	Evergreen.	Light to full.	To 3 ft, erect, spreading.	Fronds to 2 ft long, finely divided, reddish when unfurling, later turning deep green. Leaflets toothed.	Drought tolerant, hardy. Use as accent plant in landscape.
Humata tyermannii Bear's-Foot Fern	10 B,C,J	Deciduous.	Light to full.	To 1 ft, creeping.	Rhizomes covered with white, shiny, scale-like hairs, hence its name. Fronds to 12 in. long, finely divided, growing from rhizome.	Usually grown as houseplant, in hanging baskets. Brownish rhizomes indicate overwatering.
Matteuccia struthiopteris Ostrich Fern	3-8 A,B,F,G,H,I	Evergreen.	Light to full.	To 5 ft, upright, vase shaped.	Fronds plumelike, to 5 ft long, once-divided, dark green with toothed leaflets.	Because of size, recommended for outdoors only. Hardy native. Use for background or specimen against fence, wall.
Microlepia strigosa Lace Fern	9-10 B,C,J	Evergreen.	Light to half.	To 3 ft, mounding.	Rhizomes clumplike. Fronds to 3 ft long, 1 ft wide, finely divided, light green.	Divide rhizomes at end of growing season. Can be grown in containers.
Nephrolepis exaltata Sword Fern	10 C,J	Evergreen.	Light to full.	To 5 ft, erect.	Fronds to 5 ft long, 6 in. wide, once-divided, bright green. Leaflets sometimes toothed.	Many cultivars available. Effective in pots raised on plantstands for arching fronds to be appreciated. *N. exaltata* 'Bostoniensis' (Boston Fern): wider, more arching fronds.

Maidenhair fern (*Adiantum pedatum*) lends itself well to many different uses in a variety of situations and thrives in varying degrees of shade.

Sword fern (*Nephrolepis exaltata*) is widely grown in shade gardens in regions where the climate is mild year round.

Botanical/Common Name	Zones and Regions	Evergreen/Deciduous	Type of Shade	Size and Form	Plant Description	Comments/Uses
Osmunda cinnamomea — Cinnamon Fern, Fiddleheads	3-8 A,B,F, G,H,I	Deciduous.	Light to full.	To 5 ft, vase shaped.	Two types of fronds: sterile—to 5 ft long, twice-divided, green. Fertile—arise from center of plant, leaflets compact near stem, turning brown.	Fertile fronds turn brown and wither early. Can take sun if kept moist. Young, expanding fronds edible, arising very early in spring. Use for background.
O. regalis — Royal Fern, Flowering Fern	3-10 All regions.	Deciduous.	Light to full.	To 6 ft, spreading, vase shaped.	Fronds to 6 ft, twice-divided, toothed leaflets, expanding in shades of pink to yellow to red, maturing to green. Fertile leaflets brown, in clusters at end of frond.	One of the largest native ferns. Can take full sun. Use in background of shade garden. Best in cool-summer areas.
Platycerium bifurcatum — Staghorn Fern	7-10 B,C,I,J	Evergreen.	Light to half.	To 3 ft.	Two kinds of fronds: sterile—flat, overlapping, clinging tenaciously to support; fertile—growing from center of sterile fronds, to 3 ft long, leathery gray-green, forked at ends, resembling antler.	Epiphyte—usually grown on pieces of wood hung vertically to allow fronds to arch gracefully. Striking decoration for lanai, patio.
Polypodium vulgare — European Polypody, Common Polypody, Wall Fern	3-8 A,B,C, D,E,F, G,H,I	Evergreen.	Light to full.	To 1 ft, rounded.	Rhizomes form thick mats. Fronds to 2 ft long, 4 in. wide, once-divided, deep green. Leaflets with wavy edges.	One of many polypody ferns. Rhizomes edible, sweet. Many cultivars. Use in rock gardens where rhizomes creep among rocks.
Polystichum acrostichoides — Christmas Fern	3-8 A,B,E, F,G,H,I	Evergreen.	Light to full.	To 2-1/2 ft.	Fronds to 2 ft long, 5 in. wide, once-divided. Leaflets to 3 in. long with irregular bumps on upper edge, near stem.	Very popular. Used as ground cover, in woodland garden.
P. munitum — Western Sword Fern, Giant Holly Fern	7-10 A,B,C, D,E,I,J	Evergreen.	Light to full.	To 3 ft, rounded.	Fronds to 3 ft long, 10 in. wide, once-divided, leathery, dark green. Leaflets with rough edges or sharp teeth.	Many landscape uses. Mature plants may become large, with over 100 fronds.
P. setiferum — Hedge Fern, Soft Shield Fern	7-10 A,B,I,J	Evergreen.	Light to half.	To 2 ft, spreading.	Fronds arching, to 2 ft long, 6 in. wide, twice-divided, dark green.	Lacy effect. Mix with other shade-loving plants.
Rumohra adiantiformis — Leatherleaf Fern	7-10 B,C,I,J	Evergreen.	Light to half.	To 3 ft, rounded.	Fronds 3 ft long, leathery, angular in shape, finely divided. Leaflets coarsely toothed.	Can take full sun. Fronds triangular, become stiff with age. Used by florists for arrangements.
Sphaeropteris cooperi (*Alsophila australis*/*A. cooperi*) — Australian Tree Fern	9-10 B,C,J	Evergreen.	Light to half.	To 20 ft, tree fern.	Fronds to 10 ft long, fan-shaped, finely divided, light green with yellowish scale-like hairs on underside.	Fast growing. Can take full sun if kept well watered. Protect from wind. Can be grown in containers. Scalelike hairs irritating to skin.
Woodwardia fimbriata — Giant Chain Fern	7-10 A,B, C,I,J	Deciduous.	Light to full.	To 9 ft, creeping, upright.	Creeping rhizomes invasive, give rise to fronds up to 9 ft long, twice-divided. Leaflets deeply lobed.	Requires constant moisture. Fast growing when established. Interesting silhouette against wall.

Shrubs

Botanical/Common Name	Zones and Regions	Evergreen/Deciduous	Type of Shade	Size and Form	Plant Description	Comments/Uses
Abelia x grandiflora Glossy Abelia	6-10 A,B,C,D,E,G,H,I,J	Evergreen.	Half.	3 to 5 ft with equal spread. Mounding, arching branches.	Dense growth. Leaves small, glossy, opening bronzy, turning to green in summer, then reddish-brown in fall. Flowers tubular, pink to white, from summer to fall.	Use for unclipped informal hedge. 'Edward Goucher' is smaller, flowers deeper pink.
Acanthopanax sieboldianus Makino, Five-Leaved Aralia	5-10 A,B,F,G,H,I,J	Deciduous.	Light to full.	6 to 8 ft. Erect with slender, arching branches.	Spiny branches. Leaves composed of 5 leaflets. Flowers small, greenish-white, in summer.	Showy leaves make this quite useful in landscape.
Amelanchier species Serviceberry, Shadbush	4-10 A,B,F,G,H,I,J	Deciduous.	Half.	3- to 30-ft shrub or tree.	Leaves downy, clear green, turning to orange and bronze in fall. Flowers white, star-shaped bloom in early spring. Fruit dark purple or black, edible, in late spring.	Shrub or tree. Use for showy spring flower display. *A. alnifolia*: 3-20 ft, leaves 2 in. wide, serrated. *A. canadensis*: to 30 ft, berries red. *A. laevis*: to 35 ft, berries dark blue. Not for hot, dry climates.
Aronia arbutifolia Red Chokeberry	4-9 A,B,F,G,H,I,J	Deciduous.	Light to full.	6-9 ft with 3- to 5-ft spread. Open, erect habit.	Leaves to 3 in., turn rich red in fall. Small, pink-to-white flowers, in clusters bloom in spring. Fruit 1/4 in., brilliant red, in fall.	Use to brighten borders of shade gardens, woodland. Fruit holds on through fall—showy together with red leaves.
Berberis species Barberry	4-9* A,B,F,G,H,I	Deciduous or evergreen.	Light to full.	4-6 ft with equal spread. Upright, arching branches.	Spiny branches. Leaves variable in size, green turning yellow and red in fall. Flowers yellow. Blooms in spring. Berries showy in fall and winter.	Use as thorny hedge or impenetrable barrier. *B. julianae* (Zones 6-8): bluish-black berries. *B. thunbergii* (Zones 4-9): bright red berries.
Buxus species Boxwood	5-10* A,B,F,G,H,I,J	Evergreen.	Light to half.	2-20 ft with equal spread. Dense and rounded.	Dense growth. Leaves small, light green. Flowers inconspicuous.	Use for border, hedge, topiary. Protect from wind. *B. microphylla japonica* (Zones 7-10): to 5 ft unpruned, 1 ft sheared. *B. sempervirens* (Zones 5-10): to 20 ft.
Camellia species Camellia	7-10 A,B,C,I,J	Evergreen.	Light to half.	6-10 ft with equal spread. Upright.	Leaves shiny dark green. Flowers 2 to 6 in. across, red, pink, white, or any combination. Bloom season from fall through late spring.	Protect from hot sun. Full shade inhibits flowering. Use as background plant, espalier, or informal hedge. *C. japonica*: leaves large; may grow to 20 ft tall. *C. sasanqua*: leaves small; may grow to 12 ft tall.
Chaenomeles japonica Flowering Quince	5-9 A,B,D,E,F,G,H,I	Deciduous.	Light to half.	2-8 ft with equal spread. Form variable.	Thorny branches. Leaves tinged with red when young. Flowers white, pink, red, or orange. Fruit small, greenish-yellow.	Very early bloom, often in January. Use for hedge or barrier.
Chamaecyparis obtusa (dwarf forms) Dwarf Hinoki Cypress	5-9 A,B,G,H,I	Evergreen.	Half.	6 in. to 3 ft with up to 2-ft spread.	Dark green foliage is dense. Branchlets display leaves in horizontal layers.	Very slow growing, ornamental. Use for border, in rock garden.
Clethra alnifolia Summer Sweet, Sweet Pepperbush	7-10 A,B,F,G,H,I,J	Deciduous.	Light to half.	6 to 9 ft. Upright.	Dense foliage to 4 in. long, serrated. Flowers white to pink, fragrant, long lasting. Blooms in summer.	Tolerates wind, seashore conditions. Can be used as a sheared hedge.
Cornus species Dogwood	2-9* A,B,C,F,G,H,I,J	Deciduous.	Light to half.	10-20 ft. Variable spread.	Leaves to 4-5 in. long turn red in fall. Flowers surrounded by large bracts of creamy white to yellow, opening often before leaves develop. Fruit white, red, blue, or black, hanging well into winter.	*C. alba* (Zones 2-8): blood-red bark, white fruit. *C. kousa* (Zones 6-9): late blooming, red fruit. *C. mas* (Zones 4-8): scarlet-red fruit, to 3/4 in. long. *C. sanguinea* (Zones 4-7): dark red bark, black fruit. *C. stolonifera* (Zones 2-9): bright red bark in winter, white fruit.
Cotoneaster salicifolius Willow-Leafed Cotoneaster	6-10 A,B,C,E,G,H,I,J	Evergreen.	Half.	15 ft with equal spread. Arching branches.	Leaves narrow, to 3 in. long, glossy green. Flowers to 1/2 in. across, white to pinkish, early summer. Fruit round, 1/4 in., bright red.	Branches dark reddish brown, showy in fall with fruit and yellowing leaves. Use for screens or backgrounds.

Glossy abelia (*Abelia x grandiflora*)

Winter daphne (*Daphne odora*)

Wintercreeper (*Euonymus fortunei*)

Botanical/ Common Name	Zones and Regions	Evergreen/ Deciduous	Type of Shade	Size and Form	Plant Description	Comments/Uses
Cycas revoluta Sago Palm	9-10 B,C,D, I,J	Evergreen.	Light to half.	3 to 10 ft with age. Rounded.	Fernlike to palmlike. Leaves 2-3 ft long, featherlike.	Related to conifers. Very slow growing. Good for containers. Creates a tropical effect.
Daphne species Daphne	5-10* A,B,C, G,H,I,J	Evergreen or deciduous.	Light to half.*	To 4 ft, spreading wide. Form variable.	Leaves to 3 in. long, dark green. Flowers fragrant pink to purple, flowers in spring. Fruit scarlet.	Use as ground cover, in rock gardens. *D. cneorum:* (Zones 5-9) 1 ft high, spreading to 3 ft wide. *D. mezereum* (Zones 5-9): deciduous, grows to 4 ft. *D. odora* (Zones 8-10): evergreen, grows to 4 ft. Fragrance permeates garden.
Deutzia gracilis Slender Deutzia	5-8 A,B,F, G,H,I	Deciduous.	Light to full.	3 ft with 5 ft spread. Stems gracefully arching.	Leaves to 2-1/2 in. long, serrated edges. Flowers in clusters, white, in May.	Use for unclipped hedge.
Elaeagnus pungens Silverberry	7-10 A,B,C, D,H,I,J	Evergreen.	Light to half.	6-12 ft. Sprawling.	Thorny branches. Leaves to 3 in., gray-green with wavy edges. Flowers inconspicuous. Fruit oval, 1/2 in. long, red with silver bloom.	Use as clipped hedge or barrier. Variegated forms also available.
Enkianthus campanulatus Redvein Enkianthus	5-9 A,B,F, G,H,I	Deciduous.	Light.	6-20 ft, eventually half as wide. Horizontal branches.	Leaves to 3 in., dull green, with serrated edges, turns brilliant red-orange in fall. Flowers 1/2 in. long, yellow veined red. Blooms in May.	Showy clusters of bell-shaped flowers appear before leaves and good fall color make this a good choice for background plant.
Euonymus species Euonymus	3-9* All regions.	Evergreen or deciduous.	Light to half.	6-20 ft, variable spread. Compact, rounded.	Leaves to 3 in. long, deciduous types turn red in fall. Flowers inconspicuous, followed by pink, orange, or red fruit.	*E. alatus* (Zones 3-9): deciduous, to 10 ft high, equal width. Fruit red-orange. Use for hedge or screen. *E. europaea* (Zones 4-9): deciduous, to 20 ft high. Fruit pinkish, splitting open. Use singly for unusual effect. *E. japonicus* (Zones 7-9): evergreen, to 10 ft with 6-ft spread. Use as hedge or screen. *E. kiautschovica* (Zones 6-9): evergreen to 8 ft. Fruit pink, seeds red. Good formal hedge, screen, or espalier.
Fothergilla species Fothergilla	5-9 A,B,F, G,H,I	Deciduous.	Light to half.	3 to 9 ft. Form variable.	Leaves round to oval, 4 in. long. Yellow to scarlet fall color. Flowers to 2 in. across, brush-like, fragrant, white. Blooms in spring.	Use displayed in front of evergreens. *F. gardenii:* to 3 ft, flowers in spring before leaves open. *F. major:* to 9 ft, flowers in spring with opening leaves.

*Varies by species.

45

Shrubs (continued)

Botanical/Common Name	Zones and Regions	Evergreen/Deciduous	Type of Shade	Size and Form	Plant Description	Comments/Uses
Hamamelis species Witch Hazel	4-9* A,B,F, G,H,I	Deciduous.	Light to half.	6 to 30 ft. Form variable.	Leaves round, to 5 in. long, dark green above, grayish beneath, yellow in fall. Flowers 1 in. across, golden-yellow, fragrant, late winter to early spring.	Use for background. *H. mollis* (Zones 2-8): 6-10 ft, zigzag branching, blooms December to spring. *H. x intermedia*: (Zones 6-8) 15 to 18 ft, yellow flowers January to February. Showiest of witch hazels. *H. virginiana*: (Zones 4-9) 20 to 30 ft, spreading wide. Blooms October to December with yellow fall foliage.
Hibiscus syriacus Shrub Althaea, Rose-of-Sharon	5-10 A,B,E,F, G,H,I,J	Deciduous.	Light.	8-12 ft with 6-10 ft spread. Erect, round topped.	Leaves to 3 in. long, 3 lobed, coarsely toothed. Late to leaf out in spring, one of first to drop in fall. Flowers many colors, single or double, late summer until frost.	Use for unclipped hedge, screen. Tolerates seashore conditions.
Hydrangea species Hydrangea	5-10* All regions.	Deciduous.	Light to half.	6 to 20 ft. Rounded.	Dense growth. Leaves to 8 in. long. Flowers in clusters, June until frost, usually white.	Use for background, along walkways, under trees. *H. macrophylla* (Zones 6-10): blooms blue in acid soil, pink in alkaline soil. *H. arborescens* (Zones 5-9): oval leaves. *H. quercifolia* (Zones 6-9): lobed leaves turn red in fall. *H. paniculata* (Zones 5-9): grows taller, can be trained as a tree or hedge. Blooms later.
Hypericum calycinum Aaron's Beard, Creeping St.-John's-Wort	See ground covers page 55.					
Ilex species Holly	6-10* A,B,C,F, G,H,I,J	Evergreen.	Light to full.	3 to 20 ft. Form variable.	Leaves dark green, glossy, most often with spines. Flowers inconspicuous. Berries on female plants bright red, long-lasting.	Use for clipped hedges, barriers, etc. *I. aquifolium*: (Zones 6-9) to 20 ft. *I. cornuta* 'Burfordii': (Zones 6-10) to 10 ft, nearly spineless, large berries. *I. crenata*: (Zones 6-10) to 3-4 ft, berries black.
Jasminum species Jasmine	7-10* All regions.	Evergreen to semi-deciduous.	Light to half.	3 to 10 ft. Form variable.	Leaves divided into 3-5 leaflets. Flowers yellow, 1/2 in. to 2 in. across, fragrant or not, blooming throughout the year.	Use for hedges, train on trellis. *J. floridum*: (Zones 7-10) 3-4 ft, partially deciduous. *J. mesnyi*: (Zones 9-10) 6-10 ft, arching branches.
Juniperus species Juniper	2-10 All regions.	Evergreen.	Light to half.	1 to 15 ft. Form variable.	Needlelike to scalelike foliage, gray-green, blue-green, yellow-green, or dark green.	Best in full sun but tolerates partial shade. Use for ground covers, hedges, screens, windbreaks, bonsai.
Kalmia latifolia Mountain Laurel	5-9 A,B,F, G,H,I	Evergreen.	Light to full.	5 to 10 ft. Open, rounded.	Leaves oval, dark green, glossy, to 5 in. long. Flowers pinkish-white to deep pink, in clusters. Blooms late spring.	Keep mulched year round. Grows well with rhododendrons. If winter-damaged, will regrow after being cut to ground.
Kerria japonica Japanese Kerria	5-9 A,B,F, G,H,I	Deciduous.	Light to full.	6 to 8 ft with equal spread.	Green stems. Leaves to 4 in. long, coarsely toothed, turn yellow in fall. Flowers roselike, bright yellow. Blooms in spring.	Prune after flowering. Variety 'Pleniflora' has double yellow flowers. Use where full shade and poor soil exist.
Leucothoe fontanesiana Drooping Leucothoe	5-8 A,B, G,H,I	Evergreen.	Light to full.	2 to 5 ft. Arching branches.	Leaves to 6 in. long, oval, open bright green to bronze, turn purple in fall. Fragrant flowers resemble lily-of-the-valley. Blooms in spring.	Can be pruned to make high ground cover on shady slopes.
Ligustrum amurense Amur Privet	4-10 All regions.	Deciduous.	Light to half.	10 to 12 ft. Open, spreading.	Leaves 2 in. long, oval, dark green. Flowers small, creamy white, in summer. Blue-black berries follow.	Use for clipped hedge or screen. *L. obtusifolium regelianum*: to 6 ft, horizontal branching. Summer flowers white; blue-black berries follow, lasting into winter. Best deciduous privet.
Lonicera species Honeysuckle	3-10* A,B,C,F, G,H,I,J	Deciduous or evergreen.	Light to half.	6-8 ft. Form variable.	Leaves 1/2 to 3 in. long. Flowers 1/2 in. across, white to pink, fragrant, spring through summer.	*L. fragrantissima*: (Zones 6-10) deciduous, red fruit. Use as clipped hedge. *L. nitida*: (Zones 8-10) evergreen, 1/2-in.-leaves, bluish-purple fruit. *L. tatarica* (Zones 3-9) deciduous, pink flowers, red fruit. Use for screen, windbreak.

Dwarf Chinese holly (*Ilex cornuta* 'Rotunda') thrives in shade, adds evergreen beauty to the garden, and is easy to care for.

The leaves of heavenly bamboo (*Nandina domestica*) offer color interest, changing from pink to green, then to crimson and purple in winter.

As a screening plant for shaded gardens in mild climates, Japanese pittosporum (*Pittosporum tobira*) is unsurpassed.

Botanical/Common Name	Zones and Regions	Evergreen/Deciduous	Type of Shade	Size and Form	Plant Description	Comments/Uses
Magnolia virginiana Sweet Bay	6-10 A,B, H,I,J	Evergreen.	Light to half.	40 ft with 20 ft spread. Loose open habit.	Leaves to 5 in. long, grayish beneath. Flowers 3 in. across, fragrant, white, mid- to late summer. Fruit conelike, red.	Often semideciduous. Bushlike in North, more treelike in South. Use as patio tree, or single specimen.
Mahonia aquifolium Mahonia	5-9 All regions	Evergreen.	Light to half.	5 to 7 ft. Spreading.	Glossy green leaves have thorns; turn yellow and red in fall. Yellow flowers held above foliage. Blooms early spring. Berries blue-black.	Best fall color develops with some sun. Dramatic effect in landscape. Use for background, along borders.
Nandina domestica Heavenly Bamboo	6-10 A,B,C,D, E,H,I,J	Evergreen.	Light to half.	6 ft. Vertical growing.	Leaves divided into many leaflets, 1-2 in. long, opening pinkish to red, maturing to light green and turning dark red to purple in fall. Flowers small, white. Blooms in summer. Bright red berries follow.	Use for hedge, screen, containers, group plantings.
Osmanthus fragrans Sweet Olive	8-10 A,B,C,F, G,H,I,J	Evergreen.	Light to half.	To 10 ft with equal spread. Rounded.	Dense growth. Leaves oval, glossy-green, often with serrated edges, to 4 in. long. Flowers inconspicuous, white, very fragrant. Blooms spring through summer.	Can be sheared. Use for hedge, screen, in containers, or prune to small tree.
Philadelphus coronarius Mock Orange	5-8 A,B,D,	Deciduous.	Light to full.	10 to 12 ft with equal width.	Leaves oval, to 3 in. long. Flowers in clusters, 1-1/2 in. across, fragrant, white, in June.	Use for hedge, screen, or wherever fragrance is appreciated. 'Aureus': smaller, with golden leaves. Best in cool-summer climates.
Pieris species Andromeda	5-9 A,B,F, G,H,I	Evergreen.	Light to half.	3 to 10 ft. Rounded.	Leaves narrow, to 3 in. long. Flowers in clusters, white to pink.	Good companion plant for rhododendrons and azaleas. *P. floribunda*: new growth light green. Flowers white, fragrant, in spring. *P. japonica*: new growth bronzy-red. Flowers pinkish in pendulous clusters, early spring.
Pittosporum tobira Japanese Pittosporum	8-10 A,B,C, D,E,I,J	Evergreen.	Light to half.	6 to 12 ft. Broad, loose.	Leaves rounded at ends, to 4 in. long, leathery, shiny, dark green or variegated. Flowers in clusters, fragrant, creamy yellow. Blooms in early spring. Fruit round, green to brown.	Use for screens, border plantings, small tree, or in containers.

*Varies by species.

Shrubs (continued)

Botanical/Common Name	Zones and Regions	Evergreen/Deciduous	Type of Shade	Size and Form	Plant Description	Comments/Uses
Pyracantha coccinea 'Lalandei' Laland Firethorn	5-9 All regions.	Evergreen.	Light to half.	10-20 ft. Irregular form.	Thorny branches. Leaves rounded, glossy-green, to 2 in. long, 3/4 in. wide. Small, white, fragrant, flowers in clusters. Blooms in spring. Berries orange, in fall and winter.	Birds attracted to berries. Use for dense hedge, impenetrable barrier, espalier. Can train against wall. Better fruit with some sun.
Rhododendron species Azaleas and Rhododendrons	4-10 A,B,C,F, G,H,I,J	Evergreen and deciduous.	Light to full.	2-20 ft. variable.	Great variety of size and form, from low and compact to tall and open. Plants vary in leaf shape, size, and texture. Rhododendrons are generally larger shrubs, azaleas are lower and more compact with smaller leaves. Blossoms also vary in color, season, form, and number. Rhododendrons usually produce larger but fewer flower clusters. Azaleas produce an abundance of smaller flowers.	These are the most exciting spring-flowering shrubs for shady gardens. Hundreds of species and types are available. For more information see page 49. Must have acid soil and ample moisture. Colors include many shades of white, yellow, pink, red, lavender, and purple. Some are blotched or striped. Main bloom season is early-to-midspring.
Symphoricarpos albus Snowberry	3-10 All regions.	Deciduous.	Half to full.	To 6 ft, with equal spread. Arching branches.	Leaves round, to 2-1/2 in. long. Flowers in clusters, small, bell shaped, in June. Berries large, white, in fall.	Forms thicket. Birds attracted to berries. Invasive roots control erosion.
Taxus species Yew	4-9* A,B,C, D,H,I	Evergreen.	Light to full.	2 to 12 ft. Spreading.	Leaves needlelike to 2 in. long, dark green on top, light green beneath. Berries produced on female plants, red, poisonous if eaten.	*T. baccata* 'Repandens': (Zones 6-9) to 3 ft with horizontal spreading branches. *T. canadensis:* (Zones 4-9) to 3 ft, needles light green. Best for deep shade. *T. x media* 'Hatfieldii': (Zones 5-9) to 10 ft, columnar. Needles dark green. Use for hedge.
Ternstroemia gymnanthera Ternstroemia	7-10 A,B,C, D,I,J	Evergreen.	Light to full.	To 4 ft. Widespreading.	Leaves oval, to 3 in. long, bronzy when developing, red in fall and winter—especially in some sun. Flowers small, fragrant, white, in summer. Fruit yellow to orange.	Use for informal hedge. Related to camellias.
Tsuga canadensis Canadian Hemlock	5-9 A,B, G,H,I	Evergreen.	Light to full.	To 50 ft. pyramidal with drooping branches.	Leaves needlelike, dark green, 1/2 in. long. Long-lasting cones 1 in. long.	Long-lived plants. Use as hedge or screen in shady areas.
Vaccinium corymbosum Highbush Blueberry	4-8 A,B,F, G,H,I	Deciduous.	Light to half.	6 to 12 ft, with equal spread.	Leaves to 3 in. long, bluish-green when expanding in May, turning shades of yellow, bronze through red in fall. Flowers borne in profusion with expanding leaves, white. Edible dark blue berries in summer.	Must have acid soil. Prune to shape, prevent overflowering. Use fruit fresh or for pies, jams.
Viburnum species Viburnum	3-9* A,B,C,F, G,H,I,J	Deciduous.	Light to full.	4 to 15 ft. Varible widths.	Leaves to 4 in. long, dark green, serrated, turn red in fall. Small, white flowers in flat or rounded clusters, 2-4 in. across. Blooms spring or early summer. Fruit color varies, showy fall through winter. Fruit attractive to birds.	*V. acerifolium:* (Zones 3-8) to 6 ft, fruit purple-black. *V. dentatum:* (Zones 3-8) grows 10-15 ft with up to 8-ft spread. Fruit blue-black. Use as screen or background. *V. plicatum tomentosum:* (Zones 4-9) to 9 ft with equal spread, horizontal branching. Bright red fruit. *V. prunifolium:* (Zones 3-9) to 10-15 ft with equal spread, horizontal branching. Fruit blue-black. Can be trained as small tree.
Viburnum species Viburnum	7-10* A,B,C, I,J	Evergreen.	Light to full.	3 to 10 ft. Variable widths.	Leaves to 6 in. long, glossy, dark green. White flowers in clusters to 4 in. across. Blooms in spring. Fruit color varies. Showy fall through winter.	Use for informal hedges. *V. davidii:* (Zones 7-10) to 3 ft, wide spreading. Berries light blue. *V. japonicum:* (Zones 7-10) to 8 ft. Fruit red. *V. suspensum:* (Zones 9-10) to 10 ft with equal spread. Fruit red to black.

*Varies by species.

Azaleas (*Rhododendron* sp.) with their colorful flowers mix companionably with plantain lily (*Hosta* sp.) as a shade garden border.

The brilliant burst of floral color provided by azaleas (*Rhododendron* sp.) in spring transforms a shaded garden area into a dramatic garden picture.

Azaleas

Type	Zones	Evergreen or Deciduous	Comments
Belgian Indica Hybrids	8-10 Hardy to 20°F.	Evergreen.	Developed for greenhouse forcing, these plants have lush foliage and produce copious quantities of large double and semidouble flowers. Usually under 3 feet high.
Gable Hybrids	6-8 Hardy to 0°F.	Evergreen to semi-deciduous.	Hardy version of Kurume hybrids. Compact plants with heavy bloom of single or double flowers in midspring. Range from 3 to 6 feet high.
Ghent Hybrids	5-8 Hardy to −25°F.	Deciduous.	Among the most cold hardy azaleas. Single or double flowers, some fragrant, on plants about 6 feet high.
Girard Hybrids	6-8 Hardy to −5°F.	Evergreen.	Introduced in recent decades. Developed for hardiness. Double or single flowers on plants from 3 to 5 feet high.
Glenn Dale Hybrids	7-8 Hardy to 5°F.	Evergreen.	Bred primarily for hardiness. Includes a great number of varieties with differing plant sizes and flower types.
Kaempferi Hybrids	6-8 Hardy to −10°F.	Evergreen.	Vigorous upright or spreading plants reaching upwards of 6 to 8 feet high.
Knap Hill/Exbury Hybrids	5-8 Hardy to −20°F.	Deciduous.	Produce brilliantly colored, large blossoms in huge clusters. Some are fragrant. Beautiful fall color. Plants usually reach 5 to 6 feet high.
Kurume Hybrids	7-10 Hardy to 5°F.	Evergreen.	Compact plants with dense, small leaves and masses of small flowers. Branches often layered in tiers. Generally between 3 and 5 feet high.
Mollis Hybrids	5-8 Hardy to −20°F.	Deciduous.	Clusters of red, orange, or yellow flowers on 4- to 6-foot high plants. Good heat tolerance.
Rutherfordiana Hybrids	8-10 Hardy to 20°F.	Evergreen.	Originally developed for greenhouse forcing. Attractive, small bushy plants with handsome foliage and abundant single, semidouble, or double blossoms. Usually 3 to 4 feet high.
Satsuki/Macrantha Hybrids	7-10 Hardy to 5°F.	Evergreen.	Late blooming, small plants which can tolerate full sun. Large, single flowers often frilly. Seldom grow over 3 feet high.
Southern Indica Hybrids	8-10 Hardy to 20°F.	Evergreen.	Tough, outdoor, taller versions of the Belgian Indicas. Produce small to medium-sized single blossoms in midspring. Plants grow between 3 and 6 feet high and are upright or spreading. Can take full sun.

Five-leaf akebia (*Akebia quinata*) is a widely adapted vine that makes a fine shade garden ground cover when not trained to a trellis.

American bittersweet (*Celastrus scandens*) spreads quickly in a shade garden, has amber-colored autumn foliage and bright berries that are attractive after leaves fall.

Jackman clematis (*Clematis x jackmanii*) produces copious quantities of velvety-purple blooms over a long season from summer into fall.

Vines

Botanical/Common Name	Zones and Regions	Evergreen/Deciduous	Type of Shade	Size	Plant Description	Comments/Uses
Akebia quinata Five-Leaf Akebia	4-10 All regions.	Semideciduous to evergreen.	Light to half.	20 to 30 ft.	Leaves divided into 5 leaflets, 3 to 5 in. long. Dull-purple flowers in clusters, 1/2 to 1 in. across. Fruit to 4 in. long, fleshy, purple, edible.	Regrows quickly when cut to ground. Requires support or trellis to twine on.
Ampelopsis brevipedunculata Blueberry Climber	4-10 All regions.	Deciduous.	Light to half.	To 20 ft.	Leaves to 5 in. wide, 3-lobed, coarsely toothed, dark green. Flowers insignificant. Fruit berrylike, in clusters, 1/4 in. across, changing from yellow to bright blue, in fall.	Climbs by tendrils. Use against walls, provide strong support.
Aristolochia durior Dutchman's-Pipe	4-10 All regions.	Deciduous.	Light to full.	To 20 ft.	Leaves to 12 in. long, kidney-shaped, dark green. Flowers 2 to 4 in. long, shaped like a pipe, greenish-brown to purple. Blooms in summer.	Flowers hidden by large leaves. Use for covering porch or trellis, or as a screen. Often grown as an annual in mild climates.
Celastrus scandens American Bittersweet	3-9 A,B,F,G,H,I	Deciduous.	Light to half.	10 to 20 ft.	Leaves to 4 in. long, oval, light green, turning bright yellow in fall. Flowers small, greenish-white, in late spring. Yellow-and-red berries showy in fall and winter.	Climbs by twining. Invasive. Prune in early spring before leaves emerge. Use for covering trellis, fence, or arbor.
Clematis armandii Evergreen Clematis, Armand Clematis	8-10 A,B,C,D,I,J	Evergreen.	Light to half.	15 to 20 ft.	Leaves 4 to 6 in. long, divided into 3 leaflets. Flowers 1 to 2-1/2 in. across, fragrant, white, in early spring. Seedpods long, plump, in early summer.	Mulch and shade roots to keep them cool. Blooms on old wood. Prune after flowering. Use for background or accent. 'Apple Blossom' has light-pink flowers.
C. x jackmanii Jackman Clematis	5-10 A,B,C,D,F,G,H,I,J	Evergreen or deciduous.	Light to half.	12 to 15 ft.	Leaves similar to *C. armandii*. Flowers abundant, 4 to 6 in. across, flat, deep velvety-purple. Blooms from summer to fall.	Mulch and shade roots to keep them cool, moist. Blooms on new wood. Prune back to 2 ft in early spring before new growth begins. Requires support or framework. Use on arbors and trellises.
C. texensis Scarlet Clematis	4-10 All regions.	Deciduous.	Light to half.	6 to 10 ft.	Leaves divided into 3 to 8 leaflets, each 1 to 3 in. long. Flowers bell-shaped, 1 in. across, scarlet. Blooms from summer to frost. Seedpods silvery, feathery at tips, follow blossoms.	Protect from wind. Can tolerate dry periods briefly. Blooms on new wood. Prune in early spring before new growth begins. Forms a lush mass suitable for low fences.

Botanical/ Common Name	Zones and Regions	Evergreen/ Deciduous	Type of Shade	Size	Plant Description	Comments/Uses
Distictis buccinatoria Blood-Red Trumpet Vine	9-10 B,C,J	Evergreen.	Light to half.	20 to 30 ft.	Oval leaves 2 in. long. Flowers in clusters, held out from the foliage, 4 in. long, trumpet-shaped, crimson with a yellow throat. Blooms from late spring through fall.	Climbs by tendrils. Provide strong support. Use for covering fence or arbor. Prune after flowering. Tends to become top-heavy.
D. laxiflora Vanilla Trumpet Vine	9-10 B,C,J	Evergreen.	Light to half.		Leaves divided into 2 to 3 oblong leaflets, each 2-1/2 in. long. Trumpet-shaped, 3-in.-long flowers have the fragrance of vanilla and open purple, fading to orchid and white before dropping. Blooms in warm season.	Climbs by tendrils. Can bloom up to 8 months of the year in some areas. Use as a light screen for fences, against walls, or for arbors; excellent for patios where fragrance can be enjoyed.
Euonymus fortunei Wintercreeper, Evergreen Bittersweet	4-8 A,B,D, E,G,H,I	Evergreen.	Light to full.	To 20 ft.	Leaves 1 to 2 in. across, rounded to oval with scalloped margins, forming neat, glossy green carpet over branches. Mature plant has larger leaves, flowers are inconspicuous, followed by scarlet fruit.	Vines do not need support, cling by root-like holdfasts. Use for coverings walls, fences and bare ground. Many varieties available.
Hedera helix English Ivy	See ground covers, page 55, and variety chart on page 53.					
Hydrangea anomala petiolaris Climbing Hydrangea	5-9 All regions.	Deciduous.	Light to half.	To over 50 ft.	Leaves to 5 in. long, heart-shaped, fine-toothed, bright green when appearing in spring. Flowers in clusters 6 to 8 in. across, on stems 1 to 3 ft long, white, in early spring.	Climbs by aerial rootlets, clinging to almost any surface. Use for covering large surfaces such as masonry walls, tall chimneys, large trees. Support vine or it may become a rambling, creeping shrub.
Jasminum nitidum Angel-Wing Jasmine	10 B,C,D,J	Evergreen.	Light to half.	10 to 20 ft.	Leaves to 3 in. long, oval, leathery-textured, glossy. Flowers 1 to 1-1/2 in. across, shaped like pinwheels, white above, purplish underneath, fragrant, in clusters of 3. Blooms from spring through summer.	Requires support. Use as backdrop for perennial bed. Tie to an arbor or trellis, or use in containers. Prune in spring before growth begins, or after flowering in fall.
J. officinale Common White Jasmine, Poet's Jasmine	7-10 B,C,D,I,J	Semideciduous to evergreen.	Light to half.	To 30 ft.	Leaves divided into 5 to 7 leaflets, each to 2 in. long. Flowers in clusters, star-shaped, 1 in. across, very fragrant, white, bloom all summer.	Climbs by twining. Use to cover arbor or trellis. 'Aureo-variegatum' has leaves variegated yellow.
J. polyanthum Chinese Jasmine, Pink Jasmine	8-10 B,C, D,F,J	Evergreen.	Light to half.	To 20 ft.	Leaves divided into 5 to 7 lance-shaped leaflets, each to 3 in. long. Flowers small, starlike, white with rose-pink on the outside, in dense clusters on side branches.	Use for covering large fence or trellis, as ground cover, or in containers.
Lonicera hildebrandiana Giant Burmese Honeysuckle	9-10 B,C,J	Evergreen.	Light to half.	40 to 80 ft.	Leaves 4 to 6 in. long, oval, dark green. Flowers tubular, 7 in. long, fragrant, creamy white to golden yellow, in summer. Fruit small, berry-like, dark green, following blooming season.	Requires space, sturdy support. Use for espalier against fence, along tops of walls, or as ground cover on slopes. Prune after flowering.
L. japonica Japanese Honeysuckle	4-10 All regions.	Semideciduous to evergreen.	Light to half.	15 to 30 ft.	Leaves 3 in. long, oval, dark green. Flowers in pairs, 1-1/2 in. long, fragrant, purple in bud opening to white, aging to yellow. Blooms in summer.	Clings by twining; requires support. Use for fragrant screen, or unsupported to control erosion on steep slopes. 'Halliana': white flowers, leaves green, vigorous. 'Gold-Net' Honeysuckle: yellow-variegated leaves.
L. sempervirens Trumpet Honeysuckle	4-10 All regions.	Semideciduous to evergreen.	Light to half.	To 40 ft.	Leaves to 3 in. long, oval, blue-green beneath. Flowers tubular, 2 in. long, not fragrant, coral to red. Blooms throughout summer. Scarlet fruit in fall.	Climbs by twining. Use on fence or trellis for screen. Requires support, if unsupported, becomes shrubby ground cover.

Low-maintenance vines that thrive in the shade, jasmines (*Jasminum* sp.) are easy to train and bear fragrant white star-shaped flowers in summer.

A twining vine that is excellent for shade garden use, Japanese honeysuckle (*Lonicera japonica*) bears masses of fragrant blossoms in summer.

The most popular wisteria in American gardens, Chinese wisteria (*Wisteria sinensis*) is delicate in appearance, but requires a strong support.

Vines (continued)

Botanical/Common Name	Zones and Regions	Evergreen/Deciduous	Type of Shade	Size	Plant Description	Comments/Uses
Parthenocissus quinquefolia Virginia Creeper	4-10 All regions.	Deciduous.	Light to full.	To 75 ft or more.	Leaves divided into 5 leaflets, each 2 to 6 in. long with coarsely toothed margins, tinged purple when opening in spring, maturing to dark green, then turning brilliant scarlet in fall. Flowers insignificant. Fruit berrylike, bluish-black, long lasting.	Clings by adhesive disc-tipped tendrils that require rough surface. Use for covering trellis, fences, or sides of buildings. Also good ground cover for steep slopes; branches form roots.
P. tricuspidata Boston Ivy	4-10 All regions.	Deciduous.	Light to full.	To 60 ft.	Leaves 3-lobed, to 8 in. across, opening purplish, maturing to dark green, then turning fiery scarlet and yellow in fall. Flowers insignificant. Fruit berrylike, dark blue, long lasting.	More tenacious than *P. quinquefolia*, clings to almost anything. Use for covering large areas of wall, along fences or as ground cover. Tolerates dust and exhaust fumes.
Polygonum aubertii Silver Lace Vine, China Fleece Vine	5-10 All regions.	Deciduous or evergreen.	Light to half.	15 to 30 ft.	Leaves arrow-shaped, to 2 in. long, glossy with wavy margins. Flowers in dense, upright clusters, greenish-white. Blooms from late summer to fall.	Climbs by twining. Use for fence cover, patio cover, or to cascade over tops of walls. Somewhat drought tolerant.
Trachelospermum jasminoides Star Jasmine, Confederate Jasmine	8-10 B,C,D, E,I,J	Evergreen.	Light to half.	To 20 ft.	Leaves 3 in. long, oval, glossy, dark green. Flowers 1 in. across, star-shaped with twisted petals, fragrant, white, from spring through summer.	Climbs by twining. Use for covering arbors, fences, or as a screen for small gardens. Drape over walls or planters for cascading effect.
Wisteria sinensis Chinese Wisteria	5-9 All regions.	Deciduous.	Light to half.	To 25 ft.	Leaves divided into 7 to 13 leaflets, each 2 to 3 in. long. Flowers in pendulous clusters 6 to 12 in. long, slightly fragrant, blue-violet, opening simultaneously from April to May, just before leaves emerge. Seedpods velvety, 3 to 6 in., follow blossoms.	This is the most-often-seen wisteria in North American gardens. Varieties are also available with white, violet, single or double flowers. Use to twine over fence, arbor, pergola, or patio. Provide sturdy support.

English ivy (*Hedera helix*) is a hardy multipurpose evergreen vine that is unsurpassed as a lush evergreen ground cover in the shade. Enormously versatile, it can be found planted under trees, bordering a walk, or companion-planted with tender plants, such as bougainvillea (*Bougainvillea* sp.), to provide protection from frost.

Hedera helix
English Ivy

English ivy, a vining plant that is often used as a ground cover, comes in a great number of varieties that increase its usefulness in the shade garden. The varieties listed below vary in growth rate, leaf shape, and leaf color. They make excellent container subjects and their restrained growth makes them a better choice as small-scale ground covers or to create an interesting pattern on a wall or fence.

Variety Name	Description
'Aureo-variegata'	Leaves are variegated with yellow.
'Baltica'	Leaves are about half the size of the species, have whitish-green veins that pick up a purplish tinge in winter. One of the hardiest varieties.
'Bulgaria'	Cold-hardy in Zone 5 and somewhat drought-tolerant.
'California Gold'	Small light green leaves are flecked and striped yellow.
'Deltoidea'	Small medium green leaves are closely spaced and heart shaped.
'Digitata'	Leaves have 5 to 7 lobes.
'Fan'	Light green leaves with rounded lobes look like hand fans.
'Fluffy Ruffles'	Small leaves with wavy margins. Good in small spaces.
'Hahn's Self-Branching'	Small, deep green, sharply pointed leaves densely cover a compact plant. Excellent in containers or hanging baskets.
'Glacier'	Light green or gray-green, triangular leaves are edged white.
'Gold Heart'	Small green leaves with a gold or white heart in the center.
'Green Feather'	Very small, deeply cut leaves resemble a bird's foot.
'Needlepoint'	Densely branched and heavily foliaged. Dark green leaves have 3 pointed lobes.
'Sulphurea'	Slightly ruffled or curved heart-shaped leaves speckled and edged with yellow.
'238th Street'	One of the most cold hardy ivies and not subject to sunburn. Has heart-shaped leaves.

Ground Covers

Botanical/Common Name	Zones and Regions	Evergreen/Deciduous	Type of Shade	Size, Form and Planting Distance	Plant Description	Comments/Uses
Ajuga reptans Carpet Bugle, Bugleweed	4-10 A,B,C,F, G,H,I,J	Evergreen perennial.	Light to full.	6 in. high. Space plants 6 to 12 in. apart.	Spreads by runners to form a dense mat. Leaves 2 to 4 in. wide (larger in full shade) dark green, bronze, purplish, or variegated. Flowers blue, pink, or white on 6-in. spikes. Blooms in spring.	Can take full sun, especially varieties with bronze leaf tones. Use for large-scale plantings, under shade trees, along pathways.
Anemone x hybrida Japanese Anemone, Windflower	6-9 All regions.	Deciduous perennial.	Light to half.	1-2 ft high. Clumps spread to 3-4 ft. Space plants 3 to 4 ft apart.	Dark green lobed leaves form a clump. Flowers at tips of 2 to 4-ft stems, 1 to 3 in. across, single to double, white through pink to rose. Blooms in fall.	Swaying of flowers on stem-tips in breeze gives plant its name. Use along fences, walls, or foreground of tall shrubs.
Arctostaphylos uva-ursi Kinnikinick, Bearberry	2-8 A,B,C, F,G,H,I	Evergreen shrub.	Light to half.	To 10 in. high with 15-ft spread. Space plants 3 ft. apart.	Creeping branches root, forming thick mat. Leaves oval, 1 in. across, leathery, bright glossy green, turning reddish in cold weather. Flowers urn-shaped, 1/3 in. long, white to pink. Blooms in spring. Red fruit attracts birds.	Drought resistant. Use on steep slopes, trailing over walls, in rock gardens.
Asarum species Wild Ginger	4-10* A,B,F, G,H,I,J	Deciduous or evergreen perennial.	Light to full.	6 to 10 in. high with equal spread. Space plants 8 to 15 in apart.	Leaves heart-shaped, 2 to 7 in. across, green turning purple in cold weather, forming a mat. Flowers bell-shaped, purple-brown, hidden by leaves. Blooms in spring.	Requires moisture. Use combined with flowers or underneath evergreen shrubs. *A. canadense:* (Zones 4-10) Deciduous. Leaves soft, hairy. *A. caudatum:* (Zones 5-10) Evergreen. Leaves shiny, dark green. *A. europaeum:* (Zones 5-10) Evergreen leaves glossy 2 to 3 ft across.
Astilbe chinensis 'Pumila'	4-9 A,B,F, G,H,I	Deciduous perennial.	Light to half.	To 4 in. high. Wide-spreading. Space plants 1-1/2 ft apart.	Leaves to 4 in. long, serrated, forming a mat. Pink flowers in spikes to 15 in. high in summer.	Long-lasting flowers. Can be grown in containers. Especially beautiful near ponds or streams, wherever it makes a beautiful contrast to other plants.
Bergenia crassifolia Siberian Tea	4-10 A,B,C,F, G,H,I,J	Evergreen perennial.	Light to half.	To 1-1/2 ft high, rounded. Space plants 12 to 15 in. apart.	Leaves 8 in. across, leathery with wavy and serrated edges. Flowers in spikes held above foliage, white, pink or rose. Blooms in early spring.	Use for borders, rock gardens and among other shade-loving plants. Deciduous in coldest areas.
Campanula species Bellflower	3-8* A,B,C, F,G,H,I	Perennials.	Light to half.	To 1 ft high, rounded to spreading. Space plants 10 in. apart.	Leaves to 1 in. long, heart-shaped with serrated edges. Flowers bell-shaped to star-shaped, pale blue to white.	Use for small areas, bordering pathways, rock gardens. *C. elatines garganica:* (Zones 6-8) Flowers star-shaped, bright blue, summer through fall. *C. portenschlagiana:* (Zones 6-8) Flowers bell-shaped, bright blue, summer. *C. poscharskyana:* (Zones 3-8) Flowers star-shaped, blue, spring through summer.
Convallaria majalis Lily-of-the-Valley	3-7 A,B,F, G,H,I	Deciduous perennial.	Light to half.	To 10 in. high, slender, lily-like. Space "pips" 6 to 10 in. apart in clumps 1 to 2 ft apart.	Leaves to 8 in. high, 3 in. wide, dark green and tapering. White, bell-shaped, fragrant flowers on thin stalks to 8 in. Blooms in spring.	Plants spread by underground stems, dense, slow-spreading. All parts of plant poisonous. Not for mild-winter areas. Use under rhododendrons, azaleas, with ferns, at base of deciduous trees.
Epimedium species Barrenwort, Bishop's Hat	4-8 A,B,F, G,H,I	Evergreen to semi-deciduous. perennial.	Light to full.	To 15 in. high, spreading. Space plants 8 to 10 in. apart.	Leaves to 3 in. across, heart-shaped, leathery, dark green, turning reddish in fall. Flowers to 1 in., cup-shaped with a spur, various colors. Blooms in spring.	Use under trees in containers, or with ferns. Tolerates root competition. *E. grandiflorum:* Flowers white to rose. *E. pinnatum:* Flowers yellow with red spurs. *E. x youngianum* 'Niveum': Flowers pure white.
Euonymus fortunei Wintercreeper	4-8 A,B,D, E,G,H,I	Evergreen vine.	Light to full.	Vine to 1 ft high with 20-ft spread. Space plants 1 ft apart.	Leaves to 2 in. long, leathery with toothed edges, dark green. Flowers pink, insignificant.	Forms dense cover. Use for erosion control on steep slopes, banks. Can take full sun, desert heat.

In most climates, bugleweed (*Ajuga reptans*) forms a dense mat brightened by spikes of flowers in spring and early summer.

Aaron's beard (*Hypericum calycinum*) forms a low shrub brightened with yellow flowers all summer.

Ground-hugging, wide-spreading varieties of juniper (*Juniperus* sp.) make excellent ground covers for gardens in shade.

Botanical/Common Name	Zones and Regions	Evergreen/Deciduous	Type of Shade	Size, Form and Planting Distance	Plant Description	Comments/Uses
Galax urceolata (*G. aphylla*) Wandflower	4-8 A,B,F, G,H,I	Evergreen. Perennial.	Half to full.	To 6 in. high, rounded. Space plants 1 ft apart.	Spreads by underground stems. Leaves in rosettes, to 5 in. across, heart-shaped, green turning bronze in fall. White flowers on 2-1/2-ft spikes, spring through summer.	Use in rock gardens, under medium-sized shade-loving shrubs. Best in cool-summer climates.
Gaultheria procumbens Wintergreen, Teaberry, Checkerberry	4-8 A,B,F, G,H,I	Evergreen.	Light to half.	To 6 in. high with 18-in. spread. Space plants 1 to 2 ft apart.	Creeping stems give rise to woody branchlets with glossy oval, 2-in.-long leaves. Flowers small, white. Blooms in summer. Berries to 1/2 in. across, red, in fall.	Oil of wintergreen derived from leaves, fruit. Use under rhododendrons and azaleas, as ground cover in woodland gardens. Grows well with mosses.
Hedera helix English Ivy	5-10 All regions.	Evergreen vine.	Light to full.	Vine to over 50 ft. Planting variable depending on use: space close for small areas, 1-2 ft apart for large-scale covering.	Leaves to 5 in. across, leathery with 3-5 lobes, dark green. When mature, leaves heart-shaped. Flowers only on mature plants, yellow-green, 2 in. wide. Fruit similar to peas in shape, black.	Many different varieties; see page 54. Aerial rootlets on creeping stems attach plant securely to fences, walls, brick, etc. Controls erosion with deep roots. Many landscape uses.
Hosta species Plantain Lily	3-9 A,B,C, D,F,G, H,I,J	Deciduous perennial.	Half to full.	6-36 in. high, rounded to spreading. Space plants 1 to 2 ft apart.	Leaves 6-15 in. long, blue-green, heart-shaped with large, prominent veins. Flowers displayed on long spikes, lily-like, often fragrant, white through lavender to purple, in summer.	Many varieties. Very hardy plants, long-lived. Use for borders, under trees, in containers.
Hypericum calycinum Aaron's Beard, Creeping St.-John's-Wort	5-10 All regions.	Evergreen perennial.	Light to half.	To 12 in. high with equal spread. Space plants 12 to 18 in. apart.	Leaves to 4 in. long, color varies. Flowers to 3 in. across, petals bright yellow with tufts of gold-tipped yellow stamens in center.	Plants become invasive. Roots help control erosion on banks and hillsides. Mow in spring every couple of years to rejuvenate plantings.
Juniperus species Juniper	2-10 All regions.	Evergreen shrub.	Half.	4 in. to 3 ft high, wide spreading. Variable according to species. Generally 3 to 4 ft apart.	Leaves needlelike, green, blue, silver, or plumlike tints.	Heat and drought tolerant when established. Many varieties. Use as large-scale cover, in rock gardens, on hillsides, or cascading over walls.

*Varies by species.

Ground Covers (Continued)

Botanical/Common Name	Zones and Regions	Evergreen/Deciduous	Type of Shade	Size, Form and Planting Distance	Plant Description	Comments/Uses
Liriope species Lily Turf	5-10* B,C,D, G,H,I,J	Evergreen perennial	Light to half.	6 in. to 2 ft high. Grass-like clumps. Space *L. muscari*: 12-18 in. apart. *L. spicata*: 8-12 in. apart.	Leaves to 2 ft long, 1/2 in. wide. Light blue flowers on spikes 6-10 in. long. Blooms in late summer. Sparse blue-black berries follow.	Use for mass planting, edging for pathways and borders. *L. muscari*: (Zones 7-10) Leaves to 2 ft, some forms variegated. *L. spicata*: (Zones 5-10) Leaves to 10 in. long, spreads by underground stems.
Lysimachia nummularia Moneywort, Creeping Jennie	4-10 A,B,C,F, G,H,I,J	Evergreen perennial.	Light to half.	2-6 in. high with 2-ft spread. Forms dense mat. Space plants 10 to 12 in. apart.	Rooting stems. Leaves 1 in. across bright green. Flowers 3/4 in. across golden yellow. Blooms spring through summer.	Use near pools, allowing to creep over bricks and around rocks. Thrives on moisture. 'Aurea': leaves golden, takes full shade.
Mahonia repens Creeping Mahonia	4-10 All regions.	Evergreen shrub.	Light to half.	2 to 3 ft high with equal spread. Space plants 12 in. apart.	Spreads by underground runners. Leaves 2 in. long, spiny, gray-green when exiting in spring, bright red in fall, turning to bronzy-green through winter. Yellow flowers in 1-3 in. clusters. Blooms in spring. Blue-black berries attract birds.	Drought tolerant when established. Creeping underground runners help control erosion on banks, hillsides. Use for borders, around patio, in rock gardens.
Ophiopogon species Mondo Grass	6-10 B,C,D, G,H,I,J	Evergreen perennial.	Light to half.	8 in. to 3 ft high. Grass-like clumps. Space plants 6 to 12 in. apart.	Leaves to 3 ft long, 1/2 in. wide. Flowers small, white to purple, hidden by leaves, in summer. Fruit follows, pea size, dark blue.	Use for borders, under trees, in containers. *O. jaburan*: Leaves to 3 ft, some forms variegated. *O. japonicus*: Leaves 8 in. long, dark green.
Oxalis oregana Redwood Sorrel	8-10 A,B,C, I,J	Evergreen perennial.	Light to full.	10 in. high. Spreads wide. Space plants 12 to 24 in. apart.	Spreads by underground runners. Leaves divided into 3 cloverlike leaflets, 2-4 in. across, yellow green. Flowers to 1 in. across, veined petals white to pink. Blooms in spring and sometimes fall.	Moisture-loving. Goes well with ferns, underneath rhododendrons, azaleas, along shady pathways.
Pachysandra terminalis Japanese Spurge, Pachysandra	4-9 A,B,C,F, G,H,I,J	Evergreen perennial.	Light to full.	6-10 in high. Spreading. Space plants 6 to 12 in. apart.	Spreads by underground runners. Leaves 2-4 in. long, oval, veined, dark green to yellow, toothed near leaf tips. Fluffy, fragrant, white flowers on spikes. Blooms in summer. Fruit small, white, in fall.	Leaves turn yellow when exposed to full sun. Most widely planted evergreen ground cover. Use for large areas under trees, as lawn substitute.
Paxistima species Cliff-Green, Mountain-Lover, Oregon Boxwood	5-9 A,B,C,F, G,H,I,J	Evergreen shrub.	Light to half.	1 to 4 ft high, compact. Space plants 12 to 14 in. apart.	Leaves to 1 in. long, serrated toward tips, becoming bronze in fall and winter. Flowers insignificant, reddish-brown. Blooms in spring.	Excellent under azaleas and rhododendrons, around bases of trees, in rock gardens. *P. canbyi*: native to East Coast, 9-12 in. high. *P. myrsinites*: native to Pacific Northwest, 1-1/2-4 ft high and easily kept low by trimming.
Sagina species Irish Moss, Scotch Moss	4-9 A,B,C, F,G,H,I	Evergreen perennial.	Light to half.	3-4 in. high, in dense tufts. Space plants 6 in. apart.	Mosslike with slender leaves. Flowers single, up to 1/4 in. across, white.	Use between paving, under ferns, on mounds, in rock gardens, or bordering ponds. Keep free of fallen leaves or rot may occur. *S. subulata* (Irish Moss): leaves dark green. *S. subulata* 'Aurea' (Scotch Moss): leaves light green.
Sarcococca hookerana humilis Sweet Box	7-10 A,B,C, H,I	Evergreen shrub.	Light to full.	To 2 ft high, with 6-ft spread. Space plants 9 to 12 in. apart.	Spreads by underground runners. Leaves to 3 in. long, narrow, pointed, glossy, dark green. Flowers small, fragrant, white, hidden by foliage. Blooms in spring. Black berries follow.	One of the best ground covers for heavy shade. Use under trees, whenever neat, clean appearance is desired.

Redwood sorrel (*Oxalis oregana*) thrives in moist spots in shady gardens. Bright white to pink flowers are borne in spring often with a second flush of blooms in fall.

Widely adapted Irish moss (*Sagina subulata*) forms a ground-hugging carpet of lush green foliage that is attractive year round in shady sites.

Periwinkle (*Vinca minor*) is a low-maintenance ground cover outstanding for carpeting large shady areas. Lavender-blue flowers appear in spring.

Botanical/Common Name	Zones and Regions	Evergreen/Deciduous	Type of Shade	Size, Form and Planting Distance	Plant Description	Comments/Uses
Soleirolia soleirolii Baby's-Tears	8-10 B,C,D, E,I,J	Evergreen perennial.	Light to full.	1-6 in. high spreading, forming a dense carpet. Space plants 6 to 12 in. apart.	Mosslike, creeping. Leaves tiny, round, light to golden green. Flowers insignificant.	Damaged by foot traffic, but recovers rapidly. Use under ferns, rhododendrons, camellias, other shade-loving shrubs. Requires moisture.
Taxus baccata 'Repandens' Spreading English Yew	6-9 A,B,C, G,H,I	Evergreen shrub.	Light to half.	To 2 ft high with eventual 10-ft spread. Space plants 3 to 5 ft apart, if mass effect is desired.	Horizontal branching. Leaves needlelike, shiny dark green on top, white underneath. Flowers insignificant. Berries red, produced on female plants.	Both leaves and fruit are poisonous. Can use individually rather than in mass plantings. Can be made compact by pruning. Effective cascading over a wall.
Vancouveria hexandra American Barrenwort, Vancouver Fern	6-9 A,B, G,H,I	Deciduous perennial.	Light to full.	To 1 ft high. Space plants 12 to 18 in. apart.	Spreads by underground runners. Leaves divided into 3 leaflets, each to 2 in. long, apple-green. Drooping, white, 1-1/2 in. flowers on spikes held above foliage. Blooms in spring.	Leaflets have fernlike appearance, hence common name. Use with ferns under coast redwoods, oaks. Best in cool climates.
Vinca minor Periwinkle	5-10 All regions.	Evergreen perennial.	Light to full.	To 6 in. high. spreading wide. Space plants 1 ft apart.	Creeping stems form roots. Leaves to 3/4 in. long, glossy, dark green. Flowers 1 in. across, lavender-blue. Blooms in spring.	Varieties with white flowers available also. Mow periodically to force more vigorous, attractive growth. Use for large, shady areas and under trees. More restrained than its very invasive relative *V. major*.
Viola odorata Sweet Violet	See wildflowers page 41.					

*Varies by species.

St. Augustine grass (*Stenotaphrum secundatum*) grows rapidly to form a dense mat that crowds out weeds; adapted to both dry or humid areas of the southern states.

Red fescue (*Festuca rubra*) makes a choice grass for northern gardens, where it produces a deep green, fine-textured lawn under shady conditions.

Warm-Season Lawn Grasses

Warm-season grasses and dichondra grow best in regions of the southern United States with warm summers. They are dormant in winter except in frost-free areas.

Botanical Name/Common Name	Description	Comments
Dichondra micrantha Dichondra	Not a true grass. Forms a dense, low mat of small round leaves, about a 1/2 inch in diameter.	Tolerates light to half shade. Hardy to 25°F. In the Southwest and Southern California it is an indespensable lawn plant. Give ample water.
Stenotaphrum secundatum St. Augustine Grass	Light green, rough texture. Fast growing.	Excellent for half to light shade in dry or humid southern areas. Fast, tight growth crowds out weed growth. 'Floratum' resists pests and disease but isn't hardy. 'Seville' is hardier.
***Zoysia* species** Zoysia Grass	Forms a wiry, dark green mat.	Accepts light shade. Tolerates heat and drought, resists pests and disease.

Cool-Season Lawn Grasses

Cool-season grasses grow best in the cool months of spring and fall. Unless you live in a northern climate where summers are mild, cool-season grasses go dormant or grow slowly during summer. They can, however, be kept green by watering regularly in summer.

Botanical Name/Common Name	Description	Comments
Festuca rubra Red Fescue	Dependable, dark green and fine textured.	Accepts light to half shade. Dislikes heat and moist rich soil. Shade fescue (*F. rubra heterophylla*) is especially good.
Lolium perenne Turf-type Perennial Ryegrass	Dark green and fine textured.	Grows best in light to half shade and the cool summers and mild winters of coastal areas. Very quick to establish — can be walked on 3 weeks after planting. Sometimes used for winter over-seeding in southern areas.
Poa pratensis Kentucky Bluegrass	Lush dark green. Slightly bolder texture than ryegrass.	Prefers moist, mild summer areas but holds its own over most of the continent except the hottest southern areas. Best varieties for light shade include: 'Bensun' (A-34), 'Bristol', 'Eclipse', 'Glade', 'Nugget', and 'Touchdown'.

A ruggedly beautiful specimen tree, Japanese maple (*Acer palmatum*) brings richly colored leaves and a visually interesting form to shade garden situations.

Shadbush (*Amelanchier canadensis*) is a tree of many virtues for shady sites, offering star-shaped, early spring flowers, showy berries, and colorful fall foliage.

Understory Trees

Botanical/Common Name	Zones and Regions	Evergreen/Deciduous	Type of Shade	Size	Plant Description	Comments/Uses
Acer circinatum Vine Maple	6-9 A,B,G,H,I	Deciduous.	Light to full.	10 to 30 ft, depending on light, with equal spread.	Round-topped to vinelike habit. Branches often horizontal, sprawling, twisted. Leaves to 6 in. across with 7 to 11 shallow lobes. Red-tinged in spring turning to green, then yellow and orange in fall. Reddish-purple flowers in clusters, emerge before leaves appear in spring. Red-winged seed capsules are showy in fall.	Grows low, vinelike in shade, tall in sun. Can train branches to form an espalier, or place in front of dark background to display irregular structure.
A. palmatum Japanese Maple	6-8 A,B,C,F,G,H,I	Deciduous.	Light to half.	To 20 ft with equal spread.	Round-topped. Branches form close to ground. Leaves 2-4 in. long with 5-11 toothed lobes. Red-tinged, turning green, then yellow and red in fall. Some varieties have red leaves all season. Flowers insignificant.	Many varieties available. The most delicate and lacy of all maples. Protect from dry wind. Use for grove plantings, under taller trees, for entryways, near pools, as specimens.
Amelanchier canadensis Shadbush, Saskatoon, Serviceberry	4-8 A,B,F,G,H,I,J	Deciduous.	Light to half.	To 30 ft with 20-ft spread.	Round-topped, usually multi-trunked. Branches thin, graceful. Leaves round to oval, 3 in. wide, green turning to yellow, orange and red in fall. Flowers on short spikes, 1 in. across, star-shaped, in early spring before leaves expand. Fruit like miniature apples, purple-red, edible, late spring through summer.	Young leaves covered with gray down. Birds fond of berries. Effective against evergreen background when in bloom. Use under taller trees, in woodland plantings, in clumps to display bare stems.

59

Understory Trees (continued)

Botanical/Common Name	Zones and Regions	Evergreen/Deciduous	Type of Shade	Size	Plant Description	Comments/Uses
A. laevis Shadbush, Shadblow, Allegheny Serviceberry	4-8 A,B,F,G,H,I,J	Deciduous.	Light to half.	To 25 ft with 15- to 20-ft spread.	Spreading habit. Leaves oval, opening purplish, turning green, then yellow and red in fall. Fragrant, white flowers in drooping clusters. Blooms in early spring before leaves expand. Fruit bluish-purple, edible, late spring through summer.	Use similar to *A. canadensis*. You can make jams or preserves from fruit, if birds do not strip tree first.
Arbutus unedo Strawberry Tree	7-10 A,B,C,D,I,J	Evergreen.	Light to half.	10 to 35 ft with equal spread.	Rounded crown, multi-stemmed, often shrubby habit. Bark showy, red-brown, cracking. Leaves narrow, oval, 2 to 3 in. long, glossy dark green. Flowers 1/4 in. long, urn-shaped, white to pinkish, fall through winter. Fruit 3/4 in. across, yellow to red, persistant, edible but bland and mealy. Has flowers and fruits simultaneously.	Natural bonsai-like habit when mature. Fruit attracts birds. Best used where it can be looked up into.
Cercis canadensis Eastern Redbud	4-7 A,B,F,G,H,I	Deciduous.	Light.	25 to 40 ft with equal spread.	Rounded crown becomes flat-topped with age. Often multi-stemmed. Leaves 3 to 5 in. wide, heart-shaped, opening reddish-purple, turning dark green, then yellow in fall. Flowers in clusters along stems, pealike 1/2 in. across, pink to purplish-pink, in early spring before leaves.	Use for accent tree, or in group planting with dogwood—both bloom at same time. Dramatic as patio tree against light-colored background. Good in containers.
Chionanthus virginicus Fringe Tree	5-9 A,B,G,H,I,J	Deciduous.	Light to half.	To 30 ft with equal spread.	Open, spreading habit. Leaves 3 to 7 in. long. Flowers in clusters to 8 in. long, dainty with fringelike petals, fragrant, white, from late spring to early summer.	Late to leaf out in spring. Needs acid soil. Use for accent tree or in group plantings.
Cornus alternifolia Pagoda Dogwood, Green Osier	3-7 A,B,F,G,H	Deciduous.	Light to half.	To 20 ft with equal spread.	Upright habit. Branches in flat tiers, spreading horizontally. Leaves to 5 in. long, oval to pointed, expanding light green turning red in fall. Flowers in clusters, small, white, in spring. Fruit dark blue, follows flowers.	Leaves arranged opposite on stems, unique in the *Cornus* alliance. Use for unusual accent plant in woodland planting of shade garden. 'Argentea': leaves variegated white.
C. florida Flowering Dogwood	5-9 A,B,C,G,H,I,J	Deciduous.	Light to half.	20 to 40 ft with equal or slightly greater spread.	Flat-topped with horizontal spreading branches. Bark has checkered pattern. Leaves 3-6 in. long, oval, light green turning to red in fall. Flowers small, greenish-white, surrounded by large white or pink bracts 3 to 6 in. across, in spring before leaves appear.	Beautiful winter silhouette. Good as patio tree or under taller shade trees. Very showy when in bloom.
C. kousa Japanese Dogwood	6-9 A,B,C,G,H,I	Deciduous.	Light to half.	To 20 ft.	Vase-shaped when young, becoming rounded with age. Mottled bark. Flowers surrounded by large white bracts, pointed at ends. Later-blooming than flowering dogwood. Fruits, to 1 in. across, resemble raspberries.	Same landscape uses as flowering dogwood. 'Chinensis' (Chinese Dogwood): 10 to 12 ft tall, very large bracts, blooms for over 1 month.
C. mas Cornelian Cherry	4-8 A,F,G,H,I	Deciduous.	Light to full.	15 to 20 ft with equal spread.	Open, twiggy habit. Leaves 2 to 4 in. long, oval, expanding green, turning yellow to red in fall. Small yellow flowers in clusters along bare branches. Blooms very early spring. Fruit 3/4 in. across, bright scarlet, hanging like cherries, in late summer.	Fruit used in making jams and jellies. Airy habit casts light shade. Use in woodland planting in front of evergreens where bloom is best displayed. Drought tolerant.

Strawberry tree (*Arbutus unedo*) is an evergreen tree that bears tiny flowers fall into winter, bright fruit nearly year-round.

Eastern redbud (*Cercis canadensis*) can have many uses in the shade garden and is an excellent patio tree. Flowers appear before leaves emerge and foliage exhibits yellow fall color.

Japanese dogwoods (*Cornus kousa*) put on a brilliant floral show for a month in early summer.

Botanical/ Common Name	Zones and Regions	Evergreen/ Deciduous	Type of Shade	Size	Plant Description	Comments/Uses
Corynocarpus laevigata New Zealand Laurel	10 B,C,J	Evergreen.	Light to half.	20 to 30 ft with 15- to 20-ft spread.	Upright with rounded crown. Leaves to 7 in. long, oblong, leathery, glossy dark green. Flowers in small clusters, white, not showy. Fruit 1 in. across, bright orange, follows flowers, poisonous.	Slow-growing. Use for screens, hedges. Moisture-loving.
Crataegus crus-galli Cockspur Thorn	5-9 A,B,E, F,G,H,I	Deciduous.	Light.	18 to 25 ft. Wide spreading.	Flat-topped when mature. Leaves to 3 in. long, glossy dark green, turning orange-red in fall. White flowers bloom in spring. Fruit red, long lasting.	Takes well to shearing; use for hedge. Very hardy. Thorns to 3 in. long. *C. c. inermis* is thornless.
C. laevigata English Hawthorn	5-9 A,B,E, F,G,H,I	Deciduous.	Light.	18 to 25 ft with 15- to 18-ft spread.	Upright, rounded crown. Leaves variable, 2-3 in. long with 3 to 7 deep, toothed lobes. Flowers variable, single, double, white, pink, or red. Blooms in spring. Bright red fruit, summer to fall.	Use for impenetrable hedge. Not recommended for humid areas. Many varieties available.
C. phaenopyrum Washington Hawthorn	5-9 A,B,E, F,G,H,I	Deciduous.	Light.	To 30 ft with 20-ft spread.	Columnar, later developing rounded canopy. Leaves 2 to 3 in. long, glossy with 3 to 5 pointed lobes, turning scarlet to orange in fall. White flowers in clusters. Blooms in late spring. Fruit, 1/4 in. across, follows blossoms, lasting into winter.	Thorns to 3 in. long. Best hawthorn for fall color. Delicate appearance. Useful in shady lawns.
Franklinia alatamaha Franklin Tree	6-8 A,G,H,I	Deciduous.	Light.	20 to 30 ft with 10-ft spread.	Upright to pyramidal habit. Leaves 4 to 6 in. long, oval, bright green, turning orange to red in fall. Flowers camellia-like, 3 in. across, white with yellow centers. Blooms in late summer when leaves change color.	Protect from wind. Needs moist, acid soil. Often a companion for rhododendrons and azaleas. A rare and expensive tree.

American holly (*Ilex opaca*) adds evergreen beauty to shady gardens.

Japanese snowbell (*Styrax japonicus*) makes a lovely small specimen or lawn tree featuring white bell-shaped flowers in late spring; colorful foliage in fall.

Understory Trees (continued)

Botanical/Common Name	Zones and Regions	Evergreen/Deciduous	Type of Shade	Size	Plant Description	Comments/Uses
Ilex x altaclarensis 'Wilsonii' Wilson Holly	6-10 A,B,C, D,E,J,I	Evergreen.	Light to full.	To 40 ft with 30-ft spread.	Pyramidal habit. Leaves to 4-1/2 in. long, 3 in. wide, glossy green with spiny-toothed edges. Flowers insignificant. Berries bright red, abundant.	Can use for espalier or clipped hedge.
I. aquifolium English Holly, Christmas Holly	6-9 A,B,C, H,I,J	Evergreen.	Light to full.	To 35 ft with 20-ft spread.	Pyramidal habit. Leaves 1-1/2 to 3 in. long, deep glossy green. Berries on female plants bright red, abundant. Needs male and female plants for berries.	Traditional Christmas holly used for wreaths. Varieties available without spiny leaves, others variegated.
I. opaca American Holly	6-9 A,B,C, H,I,J	Evergreen.	Light to full.	To 50 ft with 30-ft spread.	Pyramidal habit. Leaves to 3 in. long, dull, dark green with spiny-toothed edges. Berries red or orange. Needs male and female plants for berries.	Varieties available without spiny leaves. Use for screens, tall hedges.
Magnolia virginiana Sweet Bay Magnolia	6-10 A,B, H,I,J	Semi-deciduous.	Light to half.	To 45 ft with 20-ft spread.	Usually multi-stemmed, dense. Leaves to 5 in. long, gray-green above, light beneath. Flowers 2-3 in. across, fragrant, creamy white. Blooms throughout the summer.	Use as patio tree. Prefers moist, acid soil.
Oxydendrum arboreum Sourwood, Sorrel Tree	6-9 A,B,G, H,I,J	Deciduous.	Light.	15 to 20 ft with 10- to 15-ft spread.	Narrow to pyramidal habit. Usually multi-trunked. Leaves 4 to 8 in. long, opening tinged red, turning dark green, then scarlet in fall. Flowers in drooping 10-in. clusters, bell-shaped, creamy white, in midsummer. Ornamental brown seedpods follow blossoms.	Requires moist, acid soil. Plant with azaleas and rhododendrons. Not for hot dry climates.
Styrax japonicus Japanese Snowbell	6-9 A,B,C, E,G,H,I	Deciduous.	Light to half.	To 30 ft.	Flat-topped with horizontal branching. Leaves to 3 in. long, oval, dark green, angling upwards. Flowers hang from undersides of branches, bell-shaped, white, from late spring to early summer.	Needs acid soil. Use as patio tree or in woodland plantings.
Tsuga canadensis Canadian Hemlock	5-9 A,B,G,H,I	Evergreen.	Light to half.	To over 60 ft.	Dense, broad, pyramidal habit. Branches droop horizontally. Dark green needlelike leaves with white stripes on the undersides, to 3/4 in. long, arranged in 2 rows on stems. Cones to 3/4 in. long, brown.	Use for trimmed hedges, screens or windbreaks. Needs acid soil.
T. caroliniana Carolina Hemlock	5-7 A,B,F, G,H,I	Evergreen.	Light to half.	40 to 70 ft.	More slender, less symmetrical than Canadian hemlock. Needles 3/4 in. long, grass-green, encircle stems. Cones 1 to 1-1/2 in. long.	Tolerant of air pollution. Uses same as Canadian hemlock. Needs acid soil.

Index

Page numbers in bold type indicate the main entry for a plant. Page numbers in italics refer to photographs or illustrations.

A Aaron's Beard, *13*, **46**, **55**
Abelia, Glossy, **44**, *45*
Abelia x grandiflora, **44**, *45*
Acanthopanax sieboldianus, **44**
Acer
  circinatum, 10, **59**
  palmatum, *10*, **11**, *17*, **59**
  platanoides, 4, 10
  saccharinum, 10
Aconite, Winter, **38**
Aconitum carmichaelii, 6, **35**, 40
Adiantum sp., 8
  pedatum, 4, 15, **42**, *43*
Agapanthus sp., **38**
Ailanthus altissima, 10
Air circulation, 26
Ajuga reptans, **54**, *55*
Akebia, Five-Leaf, **50**
Akebia quinata, **50**
Albizia julibrissin, 4, **11**
Alder, **11**
Alkanat, **35**
Alnus sp., **11**
Alsophila australis; A. cooperi. See *Sphaeropteris cooperi*.
Alyssum, Sweet, **31**
  A. saxatile. See *Aurinia*.
Amelanchier sp., **44**
  canadensis, 10, **59**
  laevis, *10*, **60**
Ampelopsis brevipedunculata, **50**
Anchusa azurea, **35**
Andromeda, *10*, **47**
Anemone, Japanese, **35**, **54**
Anemone x hybrida (A. hupensis japonica), **35**, **54**
Annuals, 30-32 (chart). See also individual plant entries.
  defined, 6
Antirrhinum majus, **30**
Aphids, 25
Aquilegia sp., 40
  x hybrida, 7, **35**
Arabis caucasica, **35**
Aralia, Five-Leaved, **44**
Arbor, 27
Arbutus unedo, 10, **60**, *61*
Arctostaphylos uva-ursi, **54**
Aristolochia durior, **50**
Aronia arbutifolia, **44**
Asarum sp., **54**
Ash, **11**
  Marshall Seedless Green, 21
  Modesto, 10
Asplenium
  bulbiferum, 8, **42**
  nidus, **42**
  trichomanes, **42**
Aster, **35**
Aster sp., **35**
Astilbe
  x. arendsii, **35**
  chinensis 'Pumila', **54**
Athyrium filix-femina, 8, **42**
Aurinia saxatilis, **35**
Azalea, 5, 8, 9, *15*, *16*, *17*, *19*, 24, **48**. See also Rhododendron.
  Evergreen, *15*, 17
  hybrids, 49 (chart)
  Knap Hill/Exbury, *19*, **49**
  Kurume, *3*, *15*, **49**

B Baby-Blue-Eyes, **31**
Baby's-Tears, **57**
Bamboo, Heavenly, *15*, **47**
Barberry, **44**
Barrenwort, **54**
  American, **57**
Basket-of-Gold, **35**
Bearberry, **54**
Beech, 4, 9
Begonia, 6
  hybrid tuberous, 33 (chart)
  Rex, **35**
  tuberous, *3*, *6*, 7, **38**
  Wax, **30**, 33 (chart)
Begonia sp., 6
  x rex-cultorum, **35**
  x semperflorens-cultorum, **30**, *33*
  x tuberhybrida, *3*, *6*, 7, *33*, **38**
Bellflower, 7, **36**, **54**
Berberis sp., **44**

Bergenia, Heartleaf, **35**
Bergenia
  cordifolia, **35**
  crassifolia, **54**
Biennials, 35-37 (chart)
Bishop's Hat, **54**
Bittersweet
  American, **50**
  Evergreen, **51**
Bleeding-Heart, **36**, 40
Bluebell, 7
Blue Bells, **38**
Bluebells, Virginia, **37**, *41*
Blueberry, Highbush, **48**
Blueberry Climber, **50**
Bluegrass, Kentucky, **58**
Bluewings, 32
Bloodroot, **41**
Botrytis, 27
Box, Sweet, **56**
Boxwobd, 16, **44**
  Oregon, **56**
Brunnera macrophylla, **36**
Bugleweed, **54**, *55*
Bugloss, **35**
  Siberian, **36**
Bulbs, 7, 8
  defined, 7
  late-spring-, summer-, fall-blooming, 39 (chart)
  planting and caring for, 27
  spring-blooming, 38-39 (chart)
  tender, 38 (chart)
Bunchberry, **40**
Buxus sp., 16, **44**

C Caladium, 15
  Fancy-Leaved, *19*, **38**, *39*
  Pink-Leaved, 15
  White-Leaved, *15*, 16
Caladium
  x hortulanum, *19*, **38**, *39*
  hybrids, 15, 16
Calla Lily, **38**
Camellia, 8, 9, *13*, 24, **44**
Camellia sp., 8, *13*, **44**
Campanula sp., 7, **36**, **54**
Candytuft, Edging, **37**
Cardinal Flower, **37**
Caring for shade gardens, 19-27. See also individual plant entries.
Carpet Bugle, **54**
Carpinus betulus, 21
Celastrus scandens, **50**
Celtis occidentalis, **11**, 21
Cercidiphyllum japonicum, **11**
Cercis canadensis, 10, *17*, **60**, *61*
Chaenomeles japonica, **44**
Chamaecyparis obtusa, **44**
Checkerberry, **55**
Chinese Pistache, **11**
Chionanthus virginicus, *10*, **60**
Chionodoxa luciliae, **38**
Chokeberry, Red, **44**
Christmas Rose, **36**
Cibotium glaucum, **42**
Cities, American, climate patterns, 22 (chart)
Cladrastis lutea, **11**, 21
Clarkia amoena, **30**
Clematis, *3*
  Armand, **50**
  Evergreen, 9, **50**
  Jackman, **50**
  Scarlet, **50**
Clematis sp., *3*
  armandii, 9, **50**
  x jackmanii, **50**
  texensis, **50**
Clethra alnifolia, **44**
Cliff-Green, **56**
Climate, 20-22. See also individual plant entries.
  altitude, 5
  climate patterns of American cities, 22 (chart)
  coolness, 6
  hardiness zones, 20 (map)
  latitude, 5
  leaf-fall and leaf-emergence dates, 21 (chart)
  microclimates, 23
  reflection of light, 5
  regional adaptation, 20, 21 (map)
  spring and fall frost dates, 22 (chart)
  sunshine percentages, 5, 22 (chart)
  temperature ranges, 22 (chart)
Clivia miniata, 7, **38**
Cockspur Thorn, **61**
Coleus, 6, **30**, *32* (leaf specimens)

Coleus x hybridus, 6, **30**
Color (design)
  all year, 15
  green gardens, 14, 15
Columbine, 7, **35**, 40
Convallaria majalis, **38**, **54**
Coralbells, **37**
Cork Tree, Amur, 7, **11**
Corm, 7
Cornelian Cherry, 10, **60**
Cornus sp., 6, 10, *28*, **44**
  alternifolia, **60**
  canadensis, **40**
  florida, 10, *17*, **60**
  kousa, *17*, **60**, *61*
  mas, 10, **60**
  stolonifera, *15*, *16*
Corynocarpus laevigata, 10, **61**
Cotoneaster, Willow-Leafed, **44**
Cotoneaster salicifolius, **44**
Crataegus sp., 10
  crus-galli, **61**
  laevigata, **61**
  phaenopyrum, **61**
Creeping Jennie, **56**
Crocus, *3*, 8, **38**
Crocus sp., *3*, 8, **38**
Cupflower, **31**
Cycas revoluta, **45**
Cyclamen, Hardy, **36**, **39**
Cyclamen sp., **36**, **39**
Cypress, Dwarf Hinoki, **44**
Cyrtomium falcatum, **42**
Cystopteris bulbifera, **42**

D Daffodil, *3*, 7, 8, *16*, **38**
Daisy, Michaelmas, **35**
Daphne, **45**
  Winter, **45**
Daphne sp., **45**
  odora, **45**
Davallia trichomanoides, **42**
Daylily, **37**
Deciduous. See Trees; individual plant entries.
Designing shade gardens, 12-17.
Deutzia, Slender, **45**
Deutzia gracilis, **45**
Dicentra sp., 40
  eximia, 40
  spectabilis, **36**
Dichondra, **58**
Dichondra micrantha, **58**
Dicksonia antarctica, **42**
Digitalis purpurea, 6, 7, **36**
Distictis
  buccinatoria, **51**
  laxiflora, **50**
Dogwood, **44**
  Flowering, *6*, 10, *17*, *28*, **60**
  Japanese, **60**
  Korean, 17
  Red-Twig, *15*, *16*
Doronicum cordatum, **36**
Dryopteris
  austriaca spinulosa, **42**
  erythrosora, **42**
Dutchman's-Pipe, **50**

E *Elaeagnus pungens*, **45**
Endymion hispanicus, **38**
Enkianthus, Redvein, **45**
Enkianthus campanulatus, **45**
Epimedium sp., **54**
Eranthis hyemalis, **38**
Erythronium dens-canis, **40**
Euonymus, **45**
  Variegated, *29*
Euonymus sp., *29*, **45**
  fortunei, *45*, **51**, **54**
Evergreen. See Trees; individual plant entries.

F *Fagus* sp., 4, 9
False Spiraea, **35**
Farewell-to-Spring, **30**
Fern, 42-43 (chart)
  Australian Tree, **43**
  Bear's-Foot, 8, **42**
  Berry Bladder, **42**
  Bird's Nest, **42**
  Christmas, **43**
  Cinnamon, 8, **43**
  Common Polypody, **43**
  European Polypody, **43**
  Fiddlehead, **43**
  Flowering, **43**
  Giant Chain, 8, **43**
  Giant Holly, **43**
  Hawaiian Tree, **42**

  Hedge, **43**
  Holly, **42**
  Japanese Shield, **42**
  Lace, **42**
  Lady, 8, **42**
  Leatherleaf, **43**
  Maidenhair, *4*, 8, 15, **42**, *43*
  Maidenhair Spleenwort, **42**
  Mother, 8, **42**
  New Zealand Tree, **42**
  Ostrich, **42**
  Royal, **43**
  Soft Shield, **43**
  Spinulose Wood, **42**
  Squirrel's-Foot, **42**
  Staghorn, 8, **43**
  Sword, 8, **42**, *43*
  Tasmanian Tree, **42**
  Toothed Wood, **42**
  Tree, 8
  Vancouver, **57**
  Wall, **43**
  Western Sword, **43**
  Wood, **42**
Fertilizing, 24, *25*
Fescue, Red, **58**
Festuca rubra, **58**
Firethorn, Laland, **48**
Fleece Vine, China, **52**
Focal points (design), 15, 16
Forget-Me-Not, **31**, *36*
Fothergilla, **45**
Fothergilla sp., **45**
Foxglove, Common, 6, 7, **36**
Franklinia alatamaha, **61**
Franklin Tree, **61**
Fraxinus sp., **11**
  pennsylvanica 'Marshall', 21
  velutina, 10
Fringe Tree, 10, **60**
Fritillaria, Crown Imperial, **39**
Fritillaria imperialis, **39**
Frost dates, 20, 22 (chart)
Fungicides, 27
Fungus diseases, 24, 27

G *Galanthus* sp., **38**
Galax urceolata (G. aphylla), **55**
Gaultheria procumbens, **55**
Geranium, **31**
  Strawberry, **37**
Ginger, Wild, **54**
Ginkgo biloba, 10, **11**
  'Fairmont', 21
Gleditsia triacanthos inermis, 4
  'Moraine', **11**, 15
Globeflower, **37**
Glory-of-the-Snow, **38**
Godetia, **30**
Golden-Rain Tree, **11**, 21
Grape Hyacinth, **38**, *39*
Grass, lawn
  cool-season, 58 (chart)
  warm-season, 58 (chart)
Ground covers, 9, 54-57 (chart). See also individual plant entries.

H Hackberry, Common, **11**, 21
Hamamelis sp., **46**
Hapu, **42**
Hardiness zones, 20 (map). See also individual plant entries.
Hawthorn, 10
  English, **61**
  Washington, **61**
Heavenly Bamboo, 15, **47**
Hedera helix, 8, 9, 10, 16, *28*, **51**, **55**
  varieties, 53 (chart)
Height and spread of plants. See individual plant entries.
Helleborus niger, **36**
Hemerocallis hybrids, **37**
Hemlock, 4
  Canadian, *16*, **48**, **62**
  Carolina, **62**
Herbaceous, defined, 6
Heuchera sanguinea, **37**
Hibiscus syriacus, **46**
Holly, 10, 24, **46**
  American, 17, *29*, **62**
  Burford, *19*
  Christmas, **62**
  Dwarf Chinese, *47*
  English, **62**
  Wilson, **62**
Honey Locust, 4
  Moraine Thornless, **11**, *15*
Honeysuckle, **46**
  Giant Burmese, **51**

63

Japanese, *19*, 52
Trumpet, 51
Hornbeam, European, 21
Hosta sp., 14, 15, **55**
sieboldiana, 15
ventricosa (*H. caerula*), 37
Humata tyermannii, 8, **42**
Hyacinth, Grape, **38**, 39
Hydrangea, **46**
Climbing, 51
Hydrangea sp., **46**
anomala petiolaris, 51
Hypericum calycinum, 13, **46**, 55

I *Iberis sempervirens*, 37
Ilex sp., 10, **46**
x. *altaclarensis* 'Wilsonii', **62**
aquifolium, **62**
cornuta
'Burfordii', *19*
'Rotunda', *47*
opaca, 17, **29**, **62**
Impatiens, 6, **30**
dwarf, 34 (chart)
intermediate, 34 (chart)
tall, 34 (chart)
White, 3
Impatiens wallerana, 3, 6, **30**, *34*
Insect problems, 27
Iris, Japanese, 37
Iris kaempferi, 37
Ivy
Boston, *13*, **51**
English, 8, 9, 10, 16, *28*, **51**, 55
varieties, 53 (chart)

J Jasmine, 9, **46**
Angel-Wing, 51
Chinese, 3, **51**
Common White, 51
Confederate, 52
Pink, 51
Poet's, 51
Star, *29*, **52**
Jasminum sp., 9, **46**, 52
nitidum, 51
officinale, 51
polyanthum, 3, **51**
Jonquil, 38
Juglans sp., 10
Juniper, **46**, 55
Juniperus sp., **46**, 55

K Kaffir Lily, 7, **38**
Kalmia latifolia, **46**
Katsura Tree, 11
Kerria, Japanese, 15, **46**
Kerria japonica, 15, **46**
Kinnikinick, 54
Koelreuteria paniculata, **11**, 21

L Lace Vine, Silver, **52**
Lath pergola, 27
Lath screen, *4*, 17
Laurel
Mountain Laurel, **46**
New Zealand, 10, **61**
Lawns, 10. See also Grass.
Leaf-fall and leaf-emergence dates, 21 (chart)
Leopard's-Bane, **36**
Leucothoe, Drooping, **46**
Leucothoe fontanesiana, **46**
Leucojum vernum, **38**
Ligustrum amurense, **46**
Lilium sp., **39**
longiflorum, 39
Lily, **39**. See also Calla; Day-; Kaffir; Magic; Plantain.
Easter, **39**
Lily-of-the-Nile, **38**
Lily-of-the-Valley, **38**, 54
Lily Turf, **56**
Linden, Little-Leaf, 11
Liriope sp., **56**
Lobelia, Edging, **30**
Lobelia
cardinalis, 37
erinus, **30**
Lobularia maritima, **31**
Lonicera sp., *19*, **46**
hildebrandiana, **51**
japonica, **51**, 52
sempervirens, **51**
Love-in-a-Mist, **31**
Lycoris squamigera, **39**
Lysimachia nummularia, **56**

M Madwort, **35**
Magic Lily, **39**

Magnolia
Southern, 4, 10
Sweet Bay, 10, **47**, **62**
Magnolia
grandiflora, 4, 10
virginiana, 10, **47**, **62**
Mahonia, **47**
Creeping, **56**
Mahonia
aquifolium, **47**
repens, **56**
Maidenhair Tree, 10, **11**
Fairmont, 21
Making people welcome (garden design), 16, 17
Makino, **44**
Maple
Japanese, *10*, **11**, *17*, **59**
Norway, 4, 10
Silver, 10
Vine, 10, **59**
Matteuccia struthiopteris, **42**
Mertensia virginica, 7, 37, **41**
Michaelmas Daisy, **35**
Microclimates, shady, 23
Microlepia strigosa, 8, **42**
Mildew, powdery, 27
Mimulus sp., **31**
Mock Orange, **47**
Mondo Grass, **56**
Moneywort, **56**
Monkey Flower, **31**
Monkshood, 6, **35**, **40**
Morus alba, 11
Moss, Irish and Scotch, **56**, *57*
Mother-of-Thousands, 37
Mountain Laurel, **46**
Mountain-Lover, **56**
Mulberry, White, 11
Mulching, 24, *25*
Muscari sp., **38**, 39
Myosotis sp., **36**
sylvatica (*M. alpestris*), **31**

N *Nandina domestica*, 15, **47**
Narcissus, **38**
Narcissus sp., 3, 7, 8, **38**
hybrids, 16
Nemophila menziesii, **31**
Nephrolepis exaltata, 8, **42**, *43*
Nerine, **39**
Nerine bowdenii, **39**
Nicotiana alata, **31**
Nierembergia sp., **31**
Nigella damascena, **31**
Nyssa sylvatica, 7, **11**

O Oak, 7
English, 11
Northern Red, 11
Scarlet, 11
Olive, Sweet, **47**
Ophiopogon sp., **56**
Orange, Mock, **47**
Ornithogalum umbellatum, **39**
Osmanthus fragrans, **47**
Osmunda
cinnamomea, 8, **43**
regalis, **43**
Oxalis oregana, **56**, *57*
Oxydendrum arboreum, 10, **62**

P Pachysandra, 8, 9, 10, **56**
Pachysandra terminalis, 8, 9, 10, **56**
Paeonia hybrids, *13*, 37
Palm, Sago, **45**
Parthenocissus sp., *13*
quinquefolia, **52**
tricuspidata, **52**
Paxistima sp., **56**
Pelargonium sp., **31**
Peony, *13*
Chinese, 37
Common Garden, 37
Pepperbush, Sweet, **44**
Perennials, 35-37 (chart). See also individual plant entries.
defined, 6, 7
Periwinkle, *3*, 8, 9, *14*, **57**
Pests, 25, 27. See also names of pests.
Petunia, **31**
Petunia x *hybrida*, **31**
Phellodendron amurense, 7, **11**
Philadelphus coronarius, **47**
Phlox, Blue, **41**
Phlox divaricata, **41**
Pieris sp., **47**
japonica, *10*
Pine, 4, 17
Pinus sp., 4, 17

Pistache, Chinese, **11**
Pistacia chinensis, **11**
Pittosporum, Japanese, **47**
Pittosporum tobira, **47**
Plane Tree, London, **11**
Plant combinations (design), 17
Plantain Lily, 14, **55**
Blue, 37
Blue-Leafed, 15
Planting. See also individual plant entries.
in compacted soil, 24
Platanus x *acerifolia*, **11**
Platycerium bifurcatum, 8, **43**
Poa pratensis, **58**
Polygonatum odoratum, 37, **41**
Polygonum aubertii, **52**
Polypodium vulgare, **43**
Polystichum
acrostichoides, **43**
munitum, **43**
setiferum, **43**
Poplar, 10
Populus sp., 10
Primrose
Fairy, **32**
Polyanthus, **32**
Primula
malacoides, **32**
x *polyantha*, **32**
Pyracantha coccinea 'Lalandei', **48**
Privet, Amur, **46**
Pruning, 26

Q *Quercus* sp., 7
coccinea, **11**
robur, **11**
rubra, **11**
Quince, Flowering, **44**

R Redbud, Eastern, 10, 17, **60**, *61*
Regional adaptation, 20, 21 (map). See also individual plant entries.
Rhizome, 7
Rhododendron, 8, 9, 16, 24, **48**. See also Azalea.
Rhododendron sp., 3, *15*; 16, *17*, *19*, **48**, *49*
hybrids, 3, 15, 16, 17, *19*
Rock Cress, **35**
Rose-of-Sharon, **46**
Rumohra adiantiformis, **43**

S Sage, Scarlet, **32**
Sagina sp., **56**
subulata, *57*
St. Augustine Grass, **58**
St.-John's-Wort, Creeping, **46**, 55
Salvia splendens, **32**
Sanguinaria canadensis, **41**
Sarcococca hookerana humilis, **56**
Saskatoon, **59**
Saxifraga stolonifera, 37
Scilla, Siberian, *14*, **39**
Scilla sp., 8
siberica, *14*, **39**
Serviceberry, **44**, **59**
Allegheny, 10, **60**
Shadblow, **60**
Shadbush, 10, **44**, **59**, **60**
Shade (deep, half, light, open), 4, 5. See also Trees; individual plant entries.
changes in, *19*, 20
creation of, *9*, 27
from deciduous trees, 20, *23*
letting in more light, 26, *27*
Shade-loving plants. See also individual plant entries.
characteristics, 6
Shrub Althaea, **46**
Shrubs, 8, 9, 44-48 (chart). See also individual plant entries.
in design, 16
growing areas, 8, 9
Siberian Tea, **54**
Silk Tree, 4, **11**
Silverberry, **45**
Snapdragon, **30**
Snowbell, Japanese, 10, **62**
Snowberry, **48**
Snowdrops, **38**
Soil, 24. See also individual plant entries.
acid (fertilizer), 24
Soleirolia soleirolii, *57*
Solomon's-Seal, 37, **41**
Sorrel, Redwood, **56**, *57*
Sorrel Tree, **62**
Sour Gum, 7, **11**
Sourwood, 10, **62**
Sphaeropteris cooperi (*Alsophila australis*; *A. cooperi*), **43**

Spread and size of plants. See individual plant entries.
Spring Snowflake, **38**
Spurge, Japanese, **56**
Squill, Siberian, **39**
Star Jasmine, *29*, **52**
Star of Bethlehem, **39**
Stenotaphrum secundatum, **58**
Strawberry Geranium, 37
Strawberry Tree, 10, **60**, *61*
Styrax japonicus, 10, **62**
Summer Sweet, **44**
Sunshine percentages, 5, 22 (chart)
Sweet Alyssum, **31**
Sweet Box, **56**
Sweet Olive, **47**
Sweet William, Wild, **41**
Symphoricarpus albus, **48**

T *Taxus* sp., **48**
baccata, 15
'Repandens', **57**
Teaberry, 55
Temperature ranges, 20, 22 (chart)
Ternstroemia, **48**
Ternstroemia gymnanthera, **48**
Texture (design), 13, 14
Thinning (pruning method), 26
Thorn, Cockspur, **61**
Tilia cordata, **11**
Tobacco
Flowering, **31**
Jasmine, **31**
Torenia fournieri, **32**
Trachelospermum sp., *29*
jasminoides, **52**
Tree-of-Heaven, 10
Trees
canopy, 10, **11**, *28*
shade-casting deciduous, 10, **11**, *23*
understory (evergreen/deciduous), 10, 59-62 (chart)
Trillium, 7
Trillium sp., 7, **41**
Trollius europaeus, 37
Trumpet Vine
Blood-Red, **50**
Vanilla, **50**
Tsuga sp., 4
canadensis, 16, **48**, **62**
caroliniana, **62**
Tuber, 7
Tulip, *14*, 16, **39**
Tulipa sp., *14*, **39**
hybrids, 16

U Uses for plants. See individual plant entries.

V *Vaccinium corymbosum*, **48**
Vancouver Fern, **57**
Vancouveria hexandra, **57**
Viburnum, *3*, **48**
Viburnum sp., *3*, **48**
Vinca minor, *3*, 8, 9, *14*, **57**
Vines, 50-52 (chart). See also individual plant entries.
creating shade with, *9*
Viola sp., 7
odorata, 37, **41**, **57**
Violet, 7
Dog-Tooth, **40**
Sweet, 37, **41**, **57**
Virginia Creeper, **52**

W Wake Robin, **41**
Walnut Tree, 10
Wandflower, **55**
Watering, 24, *25*
Wildflowers, 40-41 (chart). See also individual plant entries.
Windflower, **54**
Winter Aconite, **38**
Wintercreeper, **45**, **51**, 54
Wintergreen, **55**
Wishbone Flower, **32**
Wisteria, 9, 29
Chinese, **52**
Wisteria sp., 9, *29*
sinensis, **52**
Witch Hazel, **46**
Woodwardia fimbriata, 8, **43**

Y Yellowwood, **11**
American, 21
Yew, 15, **48**
Spreading English, **57**

Z *Zantedeschia aethiopica*, **38**
Zoysia sp., **58**
Zoysia Grass, **58**